©G.R.Tomaini 2022

Published by Pumpernickel House Publishing
through Pumpernickel House
New Orleans, Louisiana

All rights reserved.

Acknowledgements:
"Ode to Whom?" originally appeared in Outcast vol. 9
"Ode To My Butt In These Jeans" was orgiinally published by the Agapanthus Collective
"He Is Don Mosquito" and "Prometheus Rechained" were orginally published by Incognito Press
"A Love Poem By Ahab Candomblé" was orginally published by Roi Fainéant

The Rainbow Cantos

Two Attempts at
Queering The Canon

By G.R. Tomaini

To Myke

A Queer Novella In
One Hundred And Twenty Cantos

Book 1: Kiss Me, Ahab!

Contents

1   To Bacchus

3   Division I: Innocence Lost

4   A Love Poem by Ahab Candomblé
9   Ahab My Love,
10   Ahab Ruminates
10   Move-In Day I: The Boys
11   Move-In Day II: The Girls
12   Sargasso State College Convocation
12   Cultural Studies 101 I: Syllabus Week
13   Prospero Crowley Accosted
14   Brower Commons: Valhalla
14   Antigone In The Mirror
15   Alcibiades Bathing
16   Sargasso State Involvement Fair
17   Alcibiades Panting
17   Doctor de Sade's Office I: Increase In Lithium
18   Cultural Studies 101 II: Antonin Artaud
18   Office Hours I: Lilith de Sade
19   Office Hours II: Prospero Crowley
19   Alcibiades's Poetry I: Ode To My Butt In These Jeans
20   Oh, Oberon, Lord of the Fae!
20   Office Hours III: Lilith de Sade
21   The Subjugation of Alcibiades
21   Lolita Adopts Two Worms
22   Alcibiades's Poetry II: Mrs. Hendrickson Answers The Door
23   Scarlet Honor Council: The Case of Alcibiades

24 Fuck Ayn Rand: Literally!
24 Alcibiades's Poetry III: Desdemona's Secret
25 Cultural Studies 101 III: Emily Dickinson
26 A Letter To My Scumbag Son
26 Humpty Dumpty Had An Accident...
27 Gay Conversion Therapy
27 Meeting of the Leftist Society: Hadrian and Antinous Wrestle
28 One Last Hemlock Infused Scotch For Socrates
28 Alcibiades's Poetry IV: I Saw God...
29 Alcibiades's Psyche: Black and Blue
29 Winter Break: Miami Vibes
30 A Matrimony Interrupted
30 Alcibiades's Funeral Pyre
31 Alcibiades's Poetry V: Ode To Whom?
31 Oberon's Impotency
32 Office Hours IV: Lilith de Sade

35 DIVISION II: INNOCENCE INTERROGATED

36 The Fellowship of The Light
37 Something Is Rotten In The City of New Brunswick
37 Ahab 's Poetry I: Prometheus Rechained
38 Get Lolita To A Dionysian Nunnery!
38 Out of The Dark Crept Paul of Tarsus
39 Ahab 's Poetry II: He Is Don Mosquito
39 Saint Paul Bogarts The Blunt
40 Chaplain Zarathustra Blesses the Expedition
40 For Doomed Is All Love!
41 How Oberon Is A Charlatan!
41 Enter Mephistopheles, The Prince of Lies!
42 Ahab's Poetry III: The Rape of Europa By Toussaint L'Ouverture
43 The Demonic Possession of Ishmael Daedalus
44 The Withdrawal of Saint Paul
44 Rendezvous At Antinous's Childhood Treehouse

45 Prospero Crowley Consulted: Let Us Resort, Then, To Magick!
45 Lolita Takes Her Vows: Introducing Sister Lola Montez
46 And Then They Drank From The Cask of Amontillado
46 Mephisto's Presidential Proclamation I: Turn Water Into Wine!
47 Ahab's Poetry IV: El Diablo On The Runway
48 Mephisto's Presidential Proclamation II: Victorianism Is Our Cross!
49 Sermon: Thus Spoke Chaplain Zarathustra
49 Mephisto's Presidential Proclamation III: Football Is Sacred!
50 Ahab's Poetry V: Poolside Resurrection
51 Ahab Dreams of The Whale
52 Doctor de Sade's Office II: Increase In Xanax
52 The Witch Doctor Is In: I Scry The Leviathan!
53 School Newspaper: Wild Knights Have Wild Nights!
53 Ahab's Poetry VI: Papa Flee
54 And Thus, The Heart Will Break, Yet Brokenly Live On
54 Pride and Prejudice and Poppers
55 Ahab's Poetry VII: Crystalline Ballet Dancers, Three
55 Mephisto and Screwtape Sit For High Tea
56 Ahab's Poetry VIII: Fitzpatrick The Fetus Aborts Mommie Dearest
57 Sister Montez Ministers To The Nerdy
58 Ahab 's Poetry IX: Miss Betsy On Her Bench
59 A Matrimony Uninterrupted: Bells! Bells! Bells!
60 Omen: Lightning Strikes At The Ginkgo Tree
60 The Exorcism of Ishmael Daedalus
61 Alcibiades In Hell

63 **Division III: Innocence Regained**
64 Where Were You On The Ides of March, Two Thousand Twenty-One?
65 In Search of Lost Time: A Madeleine For Ahab
65 Clarissa's Poetry I: Jesus In The Bathtub
66 Mrs. Dalloway Snubs The Emperor of Ice Cream
67 Clarissa's Poetry II: Berries For Dessert
68 Nursing Home Recreation I: Mercutio The Fool
69 Flowers of Evil For A Lachrymose Ahab

70	Clarissa's Poetry III: Childbirth
71	Lolita's Archived Journal I: The Fetus That Broke The Camel's Back
72	Ahab Takes Up An Old Folio Containing Moby Dick
72	Clarissa's Poetry IV: My Real Friends
73	Lucretia Candomblé's Archived Journal I: I Will Say This Predator's Name!
74	Ahab Uses A Walker To Have Reveries of A Solitary Walker
74	Clarissa's Poetry V: No Xanax For Cicadas
75	Prune Juice For Ahab Candomblé
75	Visit From Clarissa Dalloway I: That Kiss, A Thousand Times Accursed!
76	Clarissa's Poetry VI: Five Hundred Gallons of Scotch Whiskey
76	Ahab Takes A Tumble Amidst The Ginkgo Trees
77	Alcibiades's Archived Journal I: The Grave Is A Fine And Private Place
77	Clarissa's Poetry VII: Caffeine Spinal Tap
78	Lolita's Archived Journal II: I Hear America Singing!
78	Visit From Clarissa Dalloway II: The Gates of Hell Are Open Night And Day
79	Clarissa's Poetry VIII: My God Pees On Trees
80	Clarissa Dalloway Feuds With Headmaster Svengali
80	Clarissa's Poetry IX: The Seatbelt Monster
81	Alcibiades's Archived Journal II: Dreams of A Life Spent Together
82	Visit From Clarissa Dalloway III:
82	Griefs Are A Joy Long After
83	Clarissa's Poetry X: Spider Real Estate
83	Nursing Home Recreation II: Angels In America
84	Visit From Clarissa Dalloway IV: Taste The Life Eternal!
85	Clarissa's Poetry XI: A Lost Penny!
86	Ahab Preemptively Begins His Embalming Process
86	Visit From Clarissa Dalloway V: Time Does Not Bring Relief
87	Clarissa's Poetry XII: Two Voluptuous Breasts
87	Lucretia Candomblé's Archived Journal III: Is This A Dagger I See Before Me?
88	Visit From Clarissa Dalloway VI: Do Not Go Gentle Into This Good Night!
89	Clarissa's Poetry XIII: Death of A Cell Phone
90	Ahab Is Granted A Vision of Dionysus In Mourning
90	The Angel of Death Comes For Ahab Candomblé

Bacchus, I call loud-sounding and divine,
inspiring God, a twofold shape is thine:
thy various names and attributes I sing,
o firstborn, thrice begotten, Bacchic king.
Rural, ineffable, two-formed, obscure,
two-horned, with ivy crowned, Euion pure:
bull-faced and martial, bearer of the vine,
endued with counsel prudent and divine:
Omadius, whom the leaves of vines adorn,
of Jove and Persephone occultly born
in beds ineffable; all-blessed power,
whom with triennial offerings men adore.
Immortal daemon, hear my suppliant voice,
give me in blameless plenty to rejoice;
and listen gracious to my mystic prayer,
surrounded with thy choir of nurses fair.

Orphic Hymn, c. 550-450 B. C. E.

1 Michelangelo Caravaggio, *Bacchus*

The Rainbow Cantos

---

2 John Milton, Paradise Lost

The Rainbow Cantos

A Love Poem by Ahae[3] Candomblé[4]

Only a stupid poet[5]...
could think a poem,
capable of capturing your beauty!

The honey of the beecomb,
tastes not as sweet,
as your blushing kisses.

Magnificent girl,
into the curls of your hair,
will I swirl.

Girl! Here I stand,
in your shadow,
lightened by your glimmer.

Purple majesty!
You reign over my heart,
will you care for your property?

O! Whoever had –
in his sights – a beauty[6]
such as you *to bless his eyes?*

You! What spell[7]
have you cast over me?
I am yours.

My maiden,
how much longer will you
make me wait to *love you?*

---

3   Herman Melville, *Moby Dick*; Ralph Ellison, *The Invisible Man*; James Baldwin, *Notes of A Native Son*
4   Robert A. Voeks, *Sacred Leaves of Candomblé*
5   Joyce Kilmer, *Trees*
6   Charles Baudelaire, *Beauty*
7   Nina Simone, *I Put A Spell On You*

Who birthed you ~
Aphrodite[8]*?* Beauty! ~
will you consider my outstretched hand?

Chasity, for you!
For a face as fine as yours,
will chaste I keep; *marry me?*

Where are
beauties such as you,
made? *Surely in heaven*[9]...

I thought I smelled your perfume ~
in a shopping center the other day ~
but then, it *was only a bundle of roses.*

Will your delicate hands ~
fit into this diamond ring ~
that belonged to my grandmother?

My heart flails its
vulnerable side to you ~
will you reject it?

Be with me!
Be with me forever!
I offer my soul to you ~

do you accept?

Oh good. That *trite* love poetry,
will have successfully disguised
this *urgent* plea for help...

By the time you are reading this,
it may well be too late for me!

If you're reading this ~
that means that my letter made it out;
I risked everything to get this
outside; *I only pray my captors*
don't find it first...

---

8   SANDRO BOTTICELLI, *THE BIRTH OF VENUS*

9   LANGSTON HUGHES, *HEAVEN*

The Rainbow Cantos

Here's the story – I'm being held
against my will – on a farm – somewhere
in Vermont. I can't remember where.
This place is a living hell –
I'm gnashing my teeth just
thinking about it. Every night, they
torture me – and they really enjoy it,
the *sickos*. They get off on it – they even
recorded it one time! They said they'll
play it back for me later... and that I'll
eventually grow to like it, *just like they do.*

I can't think about my pride, right now,
or about how much I've suffered
under this roof... If you want the truth
I almost wish I were *dead*. They've made
my life such a living hell – *it's gruesome.*
A few hours ago, they took my friends.
I don't know where they took them –
or what happened to them – I only know,
that whatever happened to them...
was *absolutely horrific.* I'm sorry –
I just teared a little bit –
and a few tears fell on this letter.
Please don't mind that – I can't help it.

I can barely bring myself to finish this –
I'll try to wrap it up as soon as I can.
Before you even finish reading this letter –
call the cops! I need a helicopter squad
searching for me. Make sure they have
SWAT teams search every farm in Vermont.
It's the only way they're ever going to find me.
One of my captors drives a Toyota Prius,
and the other one drives a blue minivan,
I forget which company makes it –
guess it doesn't matter too much –
so that should help narrow down their search.

Call the cops! Do it! I don't have much time left:
I can feel it. Tell them to send dog teams, too –
who knows what we're up against.

Now that you've returned to the letter –
after calling the cops – I need you to
call *all* of the major news stations
and alert them to my status...
as a prisoner against my will.
Put down this letter and do it, friend!
Now! And on second thoughts,
call the cops again – *maybe have them*

send in the air force to fly a few jets *around the tri-state area* – my captives told me that they can do a lot worse than I could ever imagine – so, we can't take *any* chances!

Hey, maybe you could even get *Spiderman to come rescue me?* That'd be cool – he's my favorite superhero. *Could you call him up?* My stupid captives won't ever let me go see his movies, even though all of my friends at school are allowed to go see them whenever they please. It took all that I could do, to persuade them to buy me the recent Spiderman action figures...

Once I got them, I played with them non-stop, and for *hours*. I kept being too tired to do my homework, so my captives eventually took my action figures away – which was a few hours ago. Now, they've got me holed up in the attic, until I have *learned my lesson* – I don't know what these *sickos* think my lesson is, but the only lessons that I *damn sure* know anything about are the ones that Mrs. Hendrickson, *who teaches the second grade at my school,* teaches me during class. *But!* my captives are really sinister – that's why I stopped calling them my parents, and started calling them my captives - I don't know what kind of lesson these *sickos* have in mind for me, but I know it won't be another *same old, same old* multiplication lesson, like the kinds Mrs. Hendrickson gives.

Those lessons are super hard – but nothing compares to the grief of losing my best friends – my superman action figures – *oh!* and let me tell you what they did to me, earlier this evening. My captives – they told me – the *sickos* – that they'd prepared a real special supper for me – *the sickos even said I would like it.* Then – they had the nerve to place a plate in front of me, *covered with sesame tofu,* and *garlic broccoli* – it makes me want to puke, *just thinking about it!*

Aw no, *I just puked all over this letter.*

The Rainbow Cantos

I don't have another sheet of paper –
so, it'll have to do. I started wailing –
I said I wouldn't eat it. Then they
freaked out – *being sickos*, after all –
and forced me to eat the broccoli...

It's difficult for me to write about!
I'm sorry, I just spilled some more tears
onto this letter. Look! *I'm sensitive!*
They can't do this to me! *It's illegal!*
I don't know what these *sickos*
think that they are doing – but I learned
about the constitution in Mrs. Hendrickson's
class – my parents can't get away with this –
please, get *Spiderman*, have him *rescue me* –
and then he'll turn my parents over
to the *coppers*, and they'll arrest these –
boogerheads! I'm kind of sleepy – *I'll finish here.*

Mommie gave me some sleepy time
milk, and it has really worn me out.
Ugh – *I loathe her* – how could she
take away my Spidermans, and
force me to eat "healthy" broccoli?
Despicable! It isn't fair, and she'll
find out the hard way – *believe me* –
when she's doing time in a federal prison.

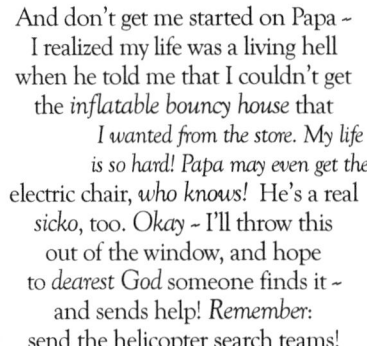

And don't get me started on Papa –
I realized my life was a living hell
when he told me that I couldn't get
the *inflatable bouncy house* that
I wanted from the store. My life
is so hard! Papa may even get the
electric chair, *who knows!* He's a real
sicko, too. Okay – I'll throw this
out of the window, and hope
to *dearest God* someone finds it –
and sends help! *Remember*:
send the helicopter search teams!

Yours fondly,

Ahab Candomblé,

Second Grade
Sargasso[10] State Preparatory Academy

---

10 Jean Rhys, *Wide Sargasso Sea*

AHAB MY LOVE,

Away fear! Away heartbreak! Away mischief!
True love[11], my true love! *Away with you!*
For there is to be no love between us!

Soulmate - tell me, do you love me?
If you love me - *then abandon me!*
Away love! Here there is no hope -

our union this very world[12] forbids!
Returned is the locket you gifted me -
forgive me! Forget me! Replace me!

[13]

---

11 The Rider-Waite Tarot Deck, The Lovers; David Lynch, What Did Jack Do?

12 The Rider-Waite Tarot Deck, The World

13 Red Rosa Luxemburg; Sigmund Freud, Fragment of An Analysis of A Case of Hysteria (Dora); Vladimir Nabokov, Lolita

The Rainbow Cantos

Ahab Ruminates

Worse than Havisham[14], she destroyed me[15]!
Sunken, sprawled out on the floor, crying -
how and why can she do this to me?

Under the harsh light of day my flesh boils[16] -
no longer will her Ginkgo[17] leaves shade my body!
How I am lost and without hope in dark woods[18]!

Without Lolita - *I am not me* - and vice versa.
My soul is extinguished; I take now a vow:
no love ever again - *it is celibacy for me!*

Move-In Day I: The Boys[19]

Swell meeting you, Ahab - Alcibiades[20], here!
He was blond, beautiful, but most of all: bold.
Shocked by a RuPaul poster, Ahab grimaced:

must I truly bunk beds with such a fairy[21]?
Ahab could be kind of cute, thought Alcibiades:
caramel skin, candy-apple lips, with sooty curls.

Woe is me: I left my Xbox360[22] far away at home!
Oh no, I forgot to bring along my Hermès[23] scarf!
Thus goes the origin-story of their friendship.

---

14 Charles Dickens, *Great Expectations*; Charles Green, *Miss Havisham*
15 Johann Wolfgang van Goethe, *The Sorrows of Young Werther*
16 Stefan Lochner, *Martyrdom of Saint John the Evangelist*
17 Johann Wolfgang van Goethe, *Ginkgo Biloba*
18 Dante Alighieri, *The Inferno*
19 James Baldwin, *Giovanni's Room*
20 Plato, *The Symposium*; Anselm Feuerbach, *Agathon and Alcibiades, Symposium*
21 Charles Baudelaire, *To One Who Is Too Gay*
22 Game Device
23 Parisian Fashion House

Move-In Day II: The Girls[24]

Her perfume[25] arrived before she did:
Antigone[26]! Antigone! *Most cherished friend!*
Ah, Lolita ~ *you maneater*[27] ~ *you Jezebel*[28]!

Regale me with your tales: Venice[29] was?
Not nearly as profound as Florence[30].
In her black boots, Antigone began to dance:

all throughout Demarest did they waltz[31] ~
and no *fool*[32] set out to interrupt them:
for Demarest the dorm was open and free.

---

24   Sappho, *The Complete Poems of Sappho*
25   Charles Baudelaire, *Exotic Perfume*; Christian Dior, *Poison*
26   Sophocles, *Antigone*; G.W.F. Hegel, *Phenomenology of Mind*
27   Friedrich Wilhelm Kuhnert, *Der Menschenfresser*; Daryl Hall and John Oates, *Maneater*
28   The Bible, *First Book of Kings*; John Liston Byam Shaw, *Jezebel*
29   William Shakespeare, *The Merchant of Venice*
30   Giovanni Boccaccio, *The Decameron*
31   Theodore Roethke, *My Papa's Waltz*
32   The Rider-Waite Tarot Deck, *The Fool*

The Rainbow Cantos

Sargasso[33] State College Convocation

Hegel! Marx! Lacan[34]! Know them by heart!
Blabbed Ishmael[35] Daedalus[36], President of Sargasso State.
Ideology, he said ~ then sniffed ~ was *ubiquitous*.

Ahab clutched at his copy of *Atlas Shrugged*[37],
Antigone ~ *who saw* ~ shot him *jackal eyes*.
Lolita mustered: *Who is John Galt*[38]?

In one fell swoop Antigone took from him
his book and threw it down below them!
How else began the feud between those two?

Cultural Studies 101 I: Syllabus Week

Lilith[39] de Sade[40]. Piercing gaze[41]. Five foot nine.
Raise your hand if you have read Heidegger[42]...
Too many have not ~ *that will be a problem!*

You there ~ *speak* ~ who was Derrida[43]?
Oh, you are not omniscient? *How tragic indeed!*
Everyone listen up! Man up! *Woman up!*

You will *never* take a harder class than CS 101!
Prepare for your own *ontological obliteration*!
Your first reading shall be *Venus in Furs*[44]...

---

33   Jean Rhys, *Wide Sargasso Sea*
34   Jacques Lacan, French Psychoanalyst
35   The Bible, The Book of Genesis; Lorenzo Lippi, *Hagar and Ishmael In The Desert*; Herman Melville, *Moby Dick*
36   Lord Frederick Leighton, *Daedalus And Icarus*; James Joyce, *Portrait of The Artist As A Young Man*
37   Ayn Rand, *Atlas Shrugged*
38   Ibid
39   Dante Gabriel Rossetti, *Lady Lilith*; Howard Schwartz, *Tree of Souls: The Mythology of Judaism*
40   Marquis de Sade, *120 Days of Sodom*
41   Michel Foucault, *Discipline And Punish: The Birth of The Prison*
42   Martin Heidegger, Phenomenologist Philosopher
43   Jacques Derrida, Deconstructionist Philosopher
44   Leopold von Sacher-Masoch, *Venus in Furs*

Prospero[45] Crowley[46] Accosted

Prospero Crowley ambled directly into Ahab's leer.
By the shoulder Ahab accosted the assistant professor –
lend me your ear! *Here is my tale, here is my story*[47]!

I cannot breathe – how her tendrils[48] *asphyxiate me!*
In a sling – dangling above the void by a thread –
how she could cut me loose and *obliterate me!*

My God! *Who is this talented woman?* asked Crowley.
Reduced then to his knees, Ahab emitted a wail:
her name is Lolita Innocencia! *Her fangs pierce deep!*

---

45 William Shakespeare, *The Tempest*

46 Aleister Crowley, Magician; The Rider-Waite Tarot Deck, *The Magician*

47 Samuel Taylor Coleridge, *The Rime of The Ancient Mariner*

48 Alfred Lord Tennyson, *The Kraken*

The Rainbow Cantos

Brower Commons: Valhalla[49]

Ambrosia or espresso - or both?
Absolutely both! Fetch us some nutella, too?
You will have lobster or porterhouse, Antigone?

How rococo a dining hall, this Brower Commons!
Boys only want love if it is torture - quoth Swift[50] -
sang Lolita, planning her next victim...

Will you teach me how to love, Lolita?
Sweet Antigone, *how could I ever resist you?*
How Brower Commons is Valhalla!

Antigone In The Mirror[51]

Curse this tattered coat upon a stick[52]! *My body!*
My body but not mine! *Mirror reveal me!*
Must I have been born to be a woman?

A simple prayer: God hear me! *Change me!*
No world is this to be a woman ~
no! I shall be a man! *I said a man!*

In my dreams I escape from misogyny[53] ~
whence comes my opportunity to *metamorphosize*[54]?
God hear me! Do not abandon me! *See me!*

---

49 Richard Wagner, *The Ring Cycle*
50 Taylor Swift, *Blank Space*
51 Titian, *Woman With A Mirror*; Sylvia Plath, *Mirror*
52 W.B. Yeats, *Sailing To Byzantium*
53 Andrea Dworkin, *Woman Hating*
54 Ovid, *The Metamorphoses*; Franz Kafka, *The Metamorphosis*

Alcibiades Bathing[55]

His body: soft clay[56]; *may I be its kiln!*
Poppable sud bubbles enveloping his perfect form...
what criticism could be made of his legs?

Nor could words do justice to his countenance.
Tell me, Alcibiades, *what is it you value the most?*
I will procure it for you: *in exchange for your soul!*

Alcibiades never knew that I loved him ~
how close was that secret of secrets kept!
For, was I also looking to lose my soul?

Secret Admirer

---

55 Jacques-Louis David, *The Death of Marat*; Edgar Degas, *The Tub*; Ezra Pound, *The Bath-Tub*

56 The Bible, *The Book of Genesis*

The Rainbow Cantos

Sargasso State Involvement Fair

Come one! Come all! To the Canterbury[57] House!
Participate in our *literary salon* that meets weekly,
enticed Chaplain Trimalchio[58] Zarathustra[59], *homme de lettres*.

Literary salon! How scholarly is Sargasso State College!
Superlatively impressed, both Ahab and Alcibiades took fliers.
Meanwhile, Antigone met the Dean of Students: Dean McHavisham[60]:

so, you will join the Scarlet Honor Council[61], then, Antigone?
How could I decline the opportunity, *loving justice as I do*?
From across the gym Ahab and Antigone exchanged *rueful* glances.

---

57 Chaucer, *The Canterbury Tales*
58 Petronius, *The Satyricon*
59 Friedrich Nietzsche, *Thus Spoke Zarathustra*
60 Charles Dickens, *Great Expectations*
61 Justice Seeking Committee For Student Conduct Violations

Alcibiades Panting

A sight to see in the morning: *Alcibiades shirtless!*
Where better than Sargasso State Gardens to go for a run?
In full *bloom*[62], orchids[63] were everywhere around him.

Bang! Thunder announced its presence.
Postured[64] beneath the leaves of a Ginkgo tree ~
taking care not to get even more wet ~ *he sighed:*

Professor de Sade's class. Then homework. Then sleep.
He would have no time to go clubbing tonight!
Leaving the protection of the Ginkgo tree, *he ran home.*

Doctor de Sade[65]'s Office[66] I: Increase In Lithium[67]

Doctor de Sade could see right through Ahab, or so he thought.
Emotionally drained because he worked for CAPS[68],
de Sade's mother ~ *the famous professor* ~ had gotten him the job.

After all, he had only gone to Caribbean medical school!
His days of *sun, sand, and leisure* were long since over:
he sat behind his desk, opposite Ahab Candomblé.

We will increase your dosage of lithium: *that should work.*
How can mere pills stave off this depression? worried Ahab.
Ahab was *quadruple-polar*, because his parents were both *bipolar.*

---

62 Troye Sivan, Bloom
63 The Bible, The Book of Jeremiah
64 Patanjali, The Yoga Sutras
65 Peter Weiss, Marat/Sade; Avital Ronell, Loser Sons: Politics And Authority
66 Michel Foucault, The Birth of The Clinic: An Archeology of Medical Perception
67 Nirvana, Lithium; Shira Erlichman, Odes To Lithium
68 Counseling, Alcohol And Other Drug Assistance Program & Psychiatric Services

The Rainbow Cantos

Cultural Studies 101 II: Antonin Artaud[69]

Edvard Grieg's *Piano Concerto* mediated the silence[70]:
on the chalkboard Lilith spelled out a powerful name,
this being ~ *much to her chagrin* ~ Antonin Artaud.

Not Baudelaire! Not Rimbaud! *Only Artaud!*
As the Christian martyrs[71] taught us: *sadism is banal*[72]!
Havishamism[73] that eviscerates the emotions, *too, is trite*:

Artaud's *Theatre of Cruelty*[74] evokes the *pure* spirit of evil!
To annihilate a soul, *best to lunge for its ideology...*
Scales fell from her eyes[75] and Lolita took *vehement* notes.

Office Hours I: Lilith de Sade

You know Berlin? Have you been to Berghain[76]?
I have snorted cocaine[77] off of Derrida's *Of Grammatology*[78],
inside of that carnival of *flesh, libertinism, and festivity!*

Lilith the *Gay Scientist*[79] was startled: *for,*
if Berghain bored Alcibiades, *perhaps she would too?*
Let us change the subject: *do you know Paris*[80]?

Why, my friend was a speechwriter for Macron[81]: *how could I not?*
This was all too much for her, you see; and what of Hegel?
Coincidentally - in my view - Leibniz refutes Hegel!

---

69 French Homme De Lettres
70 Edgar Allen Poe, Sonnet - Silence
71 Charles Baudelaire, The Martyr
72 Marquis de Sade, Philosophy In The Bedroom
73 Charles Dickens, Great Expectations
74 Antonin Artaud, The Theater And Its Double
75 The Bible, The Acts Of The Apostles
76 Nightclub: Berlin, Germany
77 Eric Clapton, Cocaine
78 Jacques Derrida, Of Grammatology
79 Friedrich Nietzsche, The Gay Science
80 Charles Baudelaire, Parisian Dream
81 President of France

Office Hours II: Prospero Crowley

Antigone proposed a question to Professor Crowley:
as a Professor of Religion, have you ever heard of a Boltzman God[82]?
No: *I am but a humble specialist*, Miss Antigone.

Well, what about Boltzmann mythological creatures?
I am sorry ~ I do not see where you are going with this!
If there can be a Boltzmann God, *then there can be a Boltzmann fairy*[83]!

Do you mean to say - Antigone - that fairies may exist?
Why pray to a god when I could pray to a fairy instead?
I am sorry but that does not compute: *focus on your classwork!*

Alcibiades's Poetry I: Ode To My Butt In These Jeans

Ode To My Butt In These Jeans

Thou are not, mine ass ~
without buttress ~ worthy
of praises high; miracle
]sublime! What trick is
this? Molded between
those fibers, *black-jean*,
glory transpires; ass trod
out, and shock the world:
juicilicious, taut, marble!
Who bequeathed our race
those holy, gilded cheeks?
Immaculate folly, to wonder:
for who but Michelangelo[84]
could wrought *justice* such?

---

82 Ludwig Boltzmann, The Concept of The Boltzmann Brain

83 Edmund Spenser, The Faerie Queene; William Shakespeare, Romeo And Juliet, A Midsummer's Night Dream; Percy Bysshe Shelley, Queen Mab; Edgar Allen Poe, Fairy-Land

84 Michelangelo Buonarroti, David

The Rainbow Cantos

Oh, Oberon, Lord of the Fae![85]

4:00 A M *in Sargasso State Gardens near the fairy statue:*
candles lit, nag champa burning, garlanded and robed:
there called upon Antigone and Lolita, *Oberon, Lord of the Fae.*

On a run, Alcibiades saw them - *inquired* - and joined the effort.
Come, *Lord of the Fae*, grace us with your presence!
Poof! At three inches tall, Oberon 's voice was pleasurably deep:

who dares to interrupt my nightly decadent Tiberian[86] orgy!
Oh Oberon, *have mercy*, please forgive us our mischief!
Build for me here a fae shrine, and I shall forget this slight!

Office Hours III: Lilith de Sade

Professor deep down am I *struggling, bumbling, and bubbling!*
de Sade *appreciated* that Ahab spoke using her mannerisms;
Professor I am a disabled student with a terrible addiction!

You must let me know how I can best *satiate* your needs, Ahab!
Well Lilith - *if I may* - you see, I am addicted to my own sexuality[87]!
Oh my! And do you have a girlfriend, or any other crushes?

Lolita buckled me into a hoveround[88] and drove it off the Empire State Building!
Brushing up against him now: *if there is anything I can help you with...*
Professor, if you are trying to sexually harass me, *I may just harass you back!*

---

85 William Shakespeare, A Midsummer's Night Dream; Joseph Noel Paton, Oberon And The Mermaid
86 Emperor Tiberius
87 Wilhelm Reich, The Sexual Revolution
88 Motorized Wheelchair

The Subjugation of Alcibiades[89]

You are in for a severe *punishment*[90], said Socrates[91] McHavisham.
In tears and a tank-top, Alcibiades wondered why he had plagiarized.
This *utter deviousness* is unacceptable coming from a Sargasso State student!

Grabbing his tank-top: listen to me! *Do you hear me?*
Socrates motioned to the beating canes on the wall[92] ~
you do know what it is I am *forced* to do to you now?

Master Socrates - I am not worthy - but only say the words, and I will *subject*[93]!
Scrying from a droplet of dew, Oberon gratifiably voyeurized the event.
During it all, Alcibiades was already planning his *next* instance of plagiarism.

Lolita Adopts Two Worms[94]

Lolita needed to practice her *newfound skills* learned in de Sade's class...
Who better than two *cucks*[95] she knew: Doctor de Sade and Prospero Crowley?
Piece by piece she would deconstruct their worlds as she saw fit...

Doctor de Sade you will take this spoon and go into the bathroom, and...
obediently, de Sade *disciplined* himself with the spoon *just as instructed.*
Triumphant, Lolita said: if you *truly* want to see more of me, *you will do this*:

in size twelve font ~ *three-inch margins* ~ you will write to your *mother* ~
and inform her as to what you just did all for the sake of an *eighteen-year-old*.
And you ~ Prospero Crowley ~ what oh what shall we do with you?

---

89 German Hernández Amores, *Socrates Chiding Alcibiades in Home of a Courtesan*
90 Michel Foucault, *Discipline And Punish: The Birth of The Prison*
91 Plato, *Complete Works*; Michelangelo Caravaggio, *Socrates*
92 *American Horror Story, Asylum*
93 The Roman Catholic Mass
94 Emily Dickinson, *How Soft A Caterpillar Steps~*
95 Edward Ravenscroft, *The London Cuckolds*

ALCIBIADES'S POETRY II: MRS. HENDRICKSON ANSWERS THE DOOR[96]

Mrs. Hendrickson Answers The Door

All is well, here; *please go.*
We're not leaving until we *know for sure,*
Mrs. Hendrickson - it's our job - Doctor de Sade
asked that we confirm your *stability.*
Right, well I'm fine - *please go.*
What took you so long to open the door?
Am I a slave in my own home?
I came to the door when I *could.*
I was boiling some water, *are you satisfied?*
No need to get excited, ma'am; *how're the kids doing?*
Good. They'll be a lot better when
I can cook up some supper for them.
Speaking of which - *I need to get started -*
now could you go, *please? Please...*
A teapot whistled - *wild, screaming -*
for what seemed to be several moments.
Making tea? Let's come in for some,
and sit with you for a while?
No, I'm afraid that won't be possible -
and the water isn't for tea -
it's for their dinner, *which I need to get started.*
Fine, but we'll be back tomorrow.
Good: *here's a smile, it means I'm doing well!*
Until next we meet, boys.
Right. See you tomorrow, Mrs. Hendrickson.
Later that evening, over the sound of the
teapot screaming, a gunshot was heard -
there would be no supper for the kids that night.

---

96 SYLVIA PLATH, *LADY LAZARUS*

SCARLET HONOR COUNCIL: THE CASE OF ALCIBIADES[97]

Lenin asked: *what is to be done*[98]?; well, something needs to be done!
Alcibiades has plagiarized *seven* times now, *blabbed* Ishmael Daedalus.
Antigone willed no harm to Alcibiades: *she would vote not guilty*.

Socrates McHavisham said: *truly is Alcibiades an infernal creature!*
But have we not read Christ[99] and Derrida[100] on forgiveness?
Antigone could not agree more: *surely Alcibiades is innocent!*

I wash my hands of Alcibiades[101]! Do with him as you both will!
Ishmael left the room; *very well* ~ said Socrates ~ *here it is*:
he must do an *independent study* with me on *The Story of O*[102].

---

97 PLATO, *THE APOLOGY*

98 VLADIMIR LENIN, *WHAT IS TO BE DONE?*

99 THE BIBLE, *THE GOSPEL OF SAINT MATTHEW*

100 JACQUES DERRIDA, *ON COSMOPOLITANISM AND FORGIVENESS*

101 THE BIBLE, *THE GOSPEL OF SAINT MATTHEW*; JOSEPH MALLORD WILLIAM TURNER, *PILATE WASHING HIS HANDS*

102 ANNE DESCLOS, *THE STORY OF O*

The Rainbow Cantos

Fuck Ayn Rand[103], Literally!

Ah ~ Francis Bacon[104] ~ *the prince of all artists!*
said Ahab, taping up *Pope Innocent X*[105] to the wall.
Ahab, you do not *whine* over Lolita anymore:

what has happened to your resolve?
Alcibiades ~ *the latest fixation of my heart is Ayn Rand!*
Now that you know the truth... *do you loathe me?*

Alcibiades smiled: *how I love Milton Friedman*[106]*!*
If only Ahab were a homosexual, thought Alcibiades;
if only Alcibiades were a woman, thought Ahab.

Alcibiades's Poetry III: Desdemona's Secret[107]

Iago, my soul, never can we be together!

Take my hand as I pour out my heart:

I cannot love that brute! *My life is over.*

You must greet me in the Elysian Fields[108]...

only then may we be together! Until then:

stir up Othello's temper: *push him to the deed*;

do you really think I can live without you in my

arms, Iago? *Go forth and implement my will!*

Desdemona, how I am your vassal! *So mote it be!*

---

103 Edited By Allan Gotthelf and Gregory Salmieri, A Companion To Ayn Rand
104 Francis Bacon, Self-Portrait
105 Francis Bacon, Study After Velazquez's Portrait of Pope Innocent X
106 Libertarian Nobel Laureate In Economics; Graduate of Rutgers College
107 William Shakespeare, Othello
108 Carlos Schwabe, Elysian Fields

Cultural Studies 101 III: Emily Dickinson[109]

What is Emily Dickinson's bumblebee[110] a metaphor for?
For death - said Lolita - death-by-bee sting!
How macabre! What do you think, Antigone?

Professor de Sade, did Dickinson mean the clitoris[111]?
de Sade slapped the chalkboard in delight: *bingo!*
You're a smart girl: *take a golden sticker!*

Professor de Sade ~ I must tell the class something:
henceforward, I ~ Antigone ~ shall be Antinous[112] ~
Antinous: belted, buckled, and booted[113]!

---

109 Emily Dickinson, *The Complete Poems of Emily Dickinson*

110 Emily Dickinson, *The Murmur of The Bee*

111 Gustave Corbet, *The Origin of The World*; Georgia O'Keeffe, *Grey Lines With Black, Blue, And Yellow*; Judy Chicago, *Dinner Party*

112 Antinous, Lover of Emperor Hadrian

113 Russ Meyer, *Faster, Pussycat! Kill, Kill!*

The Rainbow Cantos

A Letter To My Scumbag Son

Undearest Ahab:

You know I only had you for the welfare check!
Now that I no longer receive it: I have no *use*[114] for you!
You will return home to find all of your belongings

thrown out of the apartment, and next to the garbage!
Do not even think about showing your face around here again!
Henceforward are you *excommunicated: you are anathema to me!*

Did you ever imagine that I cared for you, even *minutely?*
If only we could still feed *social detritus* to the lions[115]!
By the way your dog[116] is dead: *I had it put to sleep!*

Lucretia[117] *Candomblé*[118]

Humpty Dumpty[119] Had An Accident...

You said you were going to give me a blowjob[120]*!*
screamed[121] Socrates at the hapless yet handsome Alcibiades.
Things are different now: *I am besmitten with Ahab!*

Alcibiades's bruise started developing before he hit the ground.
Socrates sipped his scotch[122] and turned to go back downstairs.
Suddenly Oberon appeared on the shoulder of Alcibiades!

If you push him down the stairs, *you could always say it was me!*
Horus[123] the Egyptian god of vengeance delighted in the scene:
the once *proud* and *mighty*[124] Socrates would never walk again.

---

114 Jeremy Bentham, *The Collected Works of Jeremy Bentham*; John Stuart Mill, *Utilitarianism*
115 Roman Source of Entertainment
116 Andy Warhol, *Portrait of Maurice*
117 Euripides, *Medea*; Lucretia Borgia, *House of Borgia*; Langston Hughes, *Mother To Son*
118 Charles Baudelaire, *To A Creole Lady*
119 James William Elliott, *National Nursery Rhymes And Nursery Songs*
120 Gawker, *Mel Gibson's Phone Rants: The Complete Collection*
121 Edvard Munch, *The Scream*
122 Johnnie Walker, *Blue Label Blended Scotch Whisky*
123 Horus, *The Oxford Encyclopedia of Ancient Egypt*
124 The Rider-Waite Tarot Deck, *Strength*

GAY CONVERSION THERAPY

I believe in gay conversion therapy: *the world needs more gays!*
Antinous, truly are you our leader: *your eloquence knows no bounds!*
Alcibiades, Lolita, and Antinous formed a circle near the fae shrine:

oh Oberon! Hear our *lugubrious*[125] plight: *come to our aid!*
For you three: *what is at my disposal, is yours! Ask away!*
We have tried everything - we have even read Judith Butler[126] to him...

and yet Ahab remains a heterosexual! Convert him, we ask!
Surprised am I that the works of Judith Butler did not succeed -
very well, *so mote it be*: what was man, is now *fairy* and *poof!*

MEETING OF THE LEFTIST SOCIETY: HADRIAN[127] AND ANTINOUS WRESTLE

Karl Marx's *das Kapital*[128] is the work of a *stupid, old, and outdated fool!*
From across the room Antinous *tackled* the opinionated Hadrian...
It was not the *first time* that a fight broke out at the Leftist Society...

In fact, it would have been *odd* were there not a fight at the Leftist Society!
Uncle! Uncle! howled[129] Hadrian, *still trying to ascertain what he had said wrong...*
Once Antinous let him go, *Hadrian wrestled him back to the ground!*

Hadrian *defenestrated*[130] Antinous and jumped out the window after him -
rolling around in the grass, *and wrestling so,* their clothes ripped off of them:
the scene looked something like Edgar Degas's *Young Spartans Exercising.*

---

125 D.H. LAWRENCE
126 JUDITH BUTLER, GENDER TROUBLE
127 EMPEROR HADRIAN
128 KARL MARX, DAS KAPITAL VOLUME ONE
129 ALLEN GINSBERG, HOWL
130 THE 1618 DEFENESTRATION OF PRAGUE

The Rainbow Cantos

One Last Hemlock Infused Scotch For Socrates[131]

Socrates wake-up: *listen here – I have no further use*[132] *for your disability check.*
You cannot just throw me away – though – *for I am still a human being*[133]!
Are you afraid that you are going to die, old man? *Be more jocular!*

If I were not in this chair – but you are Socrates, you are in that chair[134]!
You gadfly! I was your daddy, I gave you everything, and –
and you abused me when I was *innocent and weak*, did you not?

Oberon whispered in Alcibiades's ear two words: *finish him!*
Let me pour you one last scotch – *with a special ingredient*, Socrates!
Quiet yourself, now: *drink of this hemlock*[135], for it is your life and salvation[136]!

Alcibiades's Poetry IV: I Saw God...[137]

I Saw God...

on the *red ass* of a baboon

while on safari one year:

how it made me believe!

---

131 Plato, Crito
132 Jeremy Bentham, The Collected Works of Jeremy Bentham; John Stuart Mill, Utilitarianism
133 Thomas Paine, Rights of Man
134 Robert Aldrich, What Ever Happened To Baby Jane?
135 Jacques-Louis David, The Death of Socrates
136 The Body and Blood of Jesus Christ
137 William Carlos Williams, The Red Wheelbarrow

Alcibiades's Psyche: Black and Blue[138]

It was not just that he beat me and persuaded me to *enjoy it*:
Socrates McHavisham burrowed himself deep into my psyche ~
if I am to love Ahab fully, *I must evacuate Socrates's hold over me...*

How could he have groomed me so, Doctor de Sade?
Already in over his head, Doctor de Sade could only respond:
Oh, yes... hmm... yes ~ what he did to you was *egregious*!

Doctor de Sade, you offer me no *balm*[139] for my wounds:
to whom or to what must I turn to rectify my damage?
Sadistically, he said: lick your chops, and turn to Jesus Christ[140]!

Winter Break: Miami Vibes

Blue skies and golden sunshine[141]: *The Sun*[142] showed up in their reading.
Deep in the ocean blue, the fishes[143] swam about:
on the beach, however, the two boys worked on their tans.

How splendorous is the gay city of Miami!
During the night-time Ahab and Alcibiades went *clubbing*.
Without a doubt, Alcibiades was still recovering from Socrates;

despite that, their Winter break vacation went *mellifluously*.
It was about that time to take things more seriously:
in Miami ~ Ahab asked Alcibiades ~ *will you marry me?*

---

138 Anna Quindlen, *Black And Blue*
139 The Bible, *The Book of Jeremiah*
140 Friedrich Nietzsche, *On The Genealogy of Morals*
141 David Lynch, *Daily Weather Report*
142 The Rider-Waite Tarot Deck, *The Sun*
143 Elizabeth Bishop, *The Fish*

The Rainbow Cantos

A Matrimony Interrupted

Asmodeus[144], *answer my call!* cried out Lilith de Sade.
Accept this sacrifice ~ *view my talisman*[145] ~ do my bidding:
on the wedding day of Alcibiades, *let him curse God and die*[146]!

It was a cheap wedding: *for*, both of them were kids.
Grieg's *Wedding Day at Troldhaugen* played on the organ;
both parties were young ~ *somewhat innocent* ~ and unafraid.

Chaplain Zarathustra presided over the simple service;
just before the kiss Asmodeus stole away Alcibiades[147]...
and then the raft broke, and the waters rushed over Ahab[148].

Alcibiades's Funeral Pyre[149]

Despite being in many wills, Alcibiades did not have one;
what possessions remained in his dorm room were claimed by family;
Ahab was beyond himself and in a most *desperate*[150] of states.

As usual, Lolita and Antinous wore garments of all black[151];
Antinous's new partner in crime ~ Hadrian ~ *did as well*.
Chaplain Zarathustra said: *Alcibiades was a man who lived and died*:

and the audience was aghast at his mimesis of *Heidegger*[152]!
Because Alcibiades was a pagan[153], he was given a funeral pyre[154]:
as the fire eclipsed Alcibiades, Ahab too felt flames: *of passion*.

---

144 The Bible, The Book of Tobit

145 The Key of Solomon, The Fifth Pentacle of Mars

146 The Bible, The Book of Job

147 Charles Baudelaire, The Death of Lovers

148 Homer, The Odyssey; Ezra Pound, The Cantos

149 Henry Wadsworth Longfellow, Tegner's Drapa

150 Gustave Corbet, The Desperate Man

151 John Singer Sargent, Portrait of Madame X; Amy Winehouse, Back To Black

152 Martin Heidegger, Grundbegriffe der aristotelischen Philosophie

153 Charles Baudelaire, The Pagan's Prayer

154 Beowulf

Alcibiades's Poetry V: Ode To Whom?

Ode To Whom?

*Here I was - going to write
an ode to you - but then I*
discovered that I could no
longer remember anything
about you; you must have
had a personality that was
not too forgettable, *maybe*
it was all my fault that you
were placed in the garbage
bin by my brain; now this
is weird - I really was set on
writing a poem about you,
but - *perhaps indeed I have!*

Oberon's Impotency

My *children*, what is amiss that you call upon me not on a Full Moon?
Have you not heard - Oberon - that your favorite - Alcibiades - lies dead?
What an infinite jest[155] - surely you mean to pull some wool over my eyes[156]?

Was not Alcibiades young and in his *prime*, and ready for *marriage*?
Oberon - his ashes lie at the bottom of the Raritan River!
Speak to us of the netherworld, Oberon: *where is Alcibiades*?

There is no such thing as the netherworld: there is only *supernaturality*.
Your riddles[157] vex us Oberon! If you are powerless in that you
may not return him to us: impotent are you *indeed*!

---

155 David Foster Wallace, Infinite Jest
156 The Bible, The Gospel of Saint Matthew
157 François-Émile Ehrmann, Oedipus And The Sphinx

The Rainbow Cantos

Office Hours IV: Lilith de Sade

Now that Alcibiades is gone: will you come home to your mother[158]?
His whole body convulsed: Ahab projectile vomited everywhere[159]!
Deeply offended, that is when de Sade's fangs came out: literally[160]!

She upturned the desk and threw Ahab up against the wall.
Fiend! What are you, and what are these teeth that you have?
You are a fool, Ahab Candomblé: and now, you must die!

As she lunged her body into his, to bite his throat -
by it seemed the *Cunning of Reason*[161] itself - a mere pencil -
in his chest pocket - pierced her heart, and she combusted thereby!

---

158 Sophocles, *Oedipus Rex*; Sigmund Freud, *The Interpretation of Dreams*
159 William Friedkin, *The Exorcist*
160 Charles Baudelaire, *The Vampire*; Bram Stoker, *Dracula*
161 G.W.F. Hegel, *Lectures On The Philosophy of History*

The Rainbow Cantos

Division II: Innocence Interrogated

The Rainbow Cantos

The Fellowship of The Light[162]

Friends, today we gather to address the elephant in the room: vampires!
Here is my testimony: in Lilith de Sade's office, I was almost her snack!
Vampires exist, my friends, that is why I have called this council!

Do you think this is funny, Ahab? I have a paper to write tonight!
If there are fairies, said Antinous, then perhaps there are vamps, too!
Exactly! I am sure they had something to do with Alcibiades's death!

These are the times that try souls[163]! Shall we do this together, then?
Let us now form the Fellowship of the Light to combat them!
Alcibiades's were the legs that launched a thousand vampire hunters[164]!

---

162 J.R.R. Tolkien, The Lord of The Rings: The Fellowship of The Ring
163 Thomas Paine, The American Crisis
164 Homer, The Iliad

Something Is Rotten In The City Of New Brunswick[165]

Ishmael *blabbed*: as President I deal with all varieties of *monsters*:
deans, professors, parents, and donors: these are my deadly foes!
But of the vampires: I knew that they existed: am I not President?

Housed at Scott Hall, the Religion Department keeps them at bay:
for beneath Scott Hall they dwell in the subterranean tunnels!
Built during the Revolutionary War by Washington, you will

need this key to unlock the hidden entrance in the basement.
Ahab took the key but as he turned to exit Ishmael *blabbed*:
not even Hercules[166], Odysseus[167], or Dante[168] would dare this quest!

Ahab's Poetry I: Prometheus Rechained[169]

Prometheus Rechained

How I am *but* a beetle on a blade of grass, sipping dew;
and you: an Athena[170] in the clouds, atop some heighted aerie!
Down from heaven you swoop to my level: *but for what purpose*?
You have come to rip up from out of me my liver? *You must be...*
just the *bird of prey* that I have sought all throughout my life!
What do you wait for? *Expose your talons! Dig them deep into me!*
Can you not see I am in *bliss*? Oh... *have I emasculated you*?
I am *Prometheus rechained*: only, *this time* Zeus did not punish me:
rather, I found my life had become *dull, monotonous,* and *regular* —
without the presence of an eagle like you, *a nemesis indeed*!

---

165 William Shakespeare, *Hamlet*

166 Ovid, *The Metamorphoses*

167 Homer, *The Odyssey*

168 Dante Alighieri, *The Inferno*

169 Aeschylus, *Prometheus Bound*; Peter Paul Rubens, *Prometheus Bound*; Percy Bysshe Shelley, *Prometheus Unbound*; Ted Hughes, *Prometheus On His Crag*

170 Gustav Klimt, *Pallas Athena*

The Rainbow Cantos

Get Lolita To A Dionysian Nunnery[171]!

Brave Ahab! Brave Antinous! Brave Hadrian!
Into the tunnels no longer with you may I go!
My heart bleeds over what onto others I have *wrought*!

No: my quest shall be not of the sword *but of the spirit*!
Talk sense to us, Lolita, *pour out to us your truth*!
Overall, the suffering I have caused: *my heart writhes*!

There is no alternative: to a Dionysian nunnery must I go!
What evil wound itself around my soul? *Ah God, I know not*[172]!
Never again shall I crave obliteration: as God is my witness[173]!

Out Of The Dark Crept Paul Of Tarsus[174]

Out of the sun and into the dark: *they reached the hidden vault*.
All of the founding members of the Fellowship of Light were there.
Into the lock went Ishmael's key: the door resembled Rodin's[175] *Gates of Hell*.

Zephyrs that smelled of *rot* and *dust* poured out of the opened vault.
Out walked a robed old man who said: *Hark! I am Paul of Tarsus*[176]!
A member of the *Guild of Alchemists*[177], I have lived longer than most...

Not all immortals are vampires then? The Fellows of Light were *shook*.
How naive of you lot: do you think that angels and demons are vampires?
In the Nethertunnels much will be *strange* to you: *let me be your guide*!

---

171 William Shakespeare, *Hamlet*

172 Robert Browning, *The Bishop Orders His Tomb At Saint Praxed's Church*

173 Saint Paul, *Epistle To The Philippians*

174 Saint Paul of Tarsus, *The New Testament*

175 Auguste Rodin, Sculptor

176 Michelangelo Caravaggio, *The Conversion of Saint Paul*; El Greco, *Saint Paul*

177 Albrecht Dürer, *Melencolia I*; Johannes Vermeer, *The Astronomer*

Ahab's Poetry II: He Is Don Mosquito[178]

He Is Don Mosquito

He flew into the
room, circling you –
his prey – just one
kiss[179], and you will
wait for him to do
it again – to fly
around your body,
taking in your scent –
serenading you –
how he is *insatiable*!
He is Don Mosquito:
he drinks your blood.

Saint Paul Bogarts The Blunt[180]

Tell us about the Nethertunnels – *what shall we be pitted up against?*
Antinous passed the blunt to Saint Paul, who thereafter *bogarted* it.
You know nothing of the tunnels – *they for span miles underground!*

Whole cities and strongholds exist within the earth – horrors abound!
What is it you intend to do? Carry out a vendetta against the vampires?
There are more of them than there are of you – *I bid you reconsider*:

justice for Alcibiades may be attained through means other than violence!
No, you say? Yet not every vampire is responsible for *grave* evils...
and Alcibiades's murder seemed to have more to do with *demons* than *vampires*!

---

178 Miguel de Cervantes, *Don Quixote*; Wolfgang Amadeus Mozart, *Don Giovanni*; Lord Byron, *Don Juan*; Moliere, *Don Juan*; Charles Baudelaire, *Don Juan In Hell*

179 Giotto di Bondone, *The Kiss of Judas*

180 Humphrey Bogart, American Thespian

The Rainbow Cantos

Chaplain Zarathustra Blesses the Expedition

Oh Dionysus, grant your blessings[181] upon this expedition!
Many a fine mead was enjoyed at the Canterbury House:
under my supervision much *merriment* shook those walls!

Now these kids who feel as though they are mine must embark –
in pursuit of justice do they intend to *crusade*[182] against vampirism;
and dear Alcibiades, *stolen from us on his own wedding day*[183]:

our hearts pound in our chests for: *Justice*[184]! Justice! Justice!
Alcibiades was not innocent, but he was young: *poor thing!*
And now into the tunnels go my children: *some may not return!*

For Doomed Is All Love!

What am I doing, saying, and thinking? thought Ahab:
for love I would one hundred thousand times circle the globe –
how I am a slave to love! Without it I shall fall down and die!

Lolita and Alcibiades fell out of my grasp – *what am I to do?*
Saint Paul – pour out your wisdom, *and I shall drink of it!*
Hold fast to your sanity, my son: *for doomed is all love!*

Never had I a love that satiated my heart: therefore, I tore it out!
Doom awaits all love[185] – *forsake your faulty motivations for this quest*:
drown love in a *well of tears*: interrogate yourself: *what drives you?*

---

181 Charles Baudelaire, *The Blessing*
182 The Children's Crusade of 1212
183 Mary Shelley, *Frankenstein; or The Modern Prometheus*
184 The Rider-Waite Tarot Deck, *Justice*
185 Saint Paul, *First Epistle To The Corinthians*

How Oberon Is A Charlatan[186]!

Saint Paul! To be your age must mean that you are *learned* in magicks!
We, too, are *wiccan*[187] practitioners: our teacher was *Oberon, Lord of the Fae.*
Paul said: *speak again*[188]: tell me of this creature: *who and what is Oberon?*

He is the Lord of the Fae: he failed us when he did not resurrect Alcibiades!
Understand: there is no such thing as fairies: Oberon is a charlatan!
Saint Paul continued: *no ~ he is either angel*[189] *or demon: let us find out!*

Seal up the tunnel: *that can wait: we must first unmask*[190] *Oberon!*
Oberon will know what killed Alcibiades: let us call upon him!
How the scales have fallen from our eyes[191]! *Off to the Fae Shrine!*

Enter Mephistopheles, The Prince of Lies![192]

In a grove of Ginkgo trees[193] lay the Fae Shrine; *summon him!* said Paul.
Oh Oberon, Lord of the Fae, we call upon you! Join us now!
Antinous! Hadrian! Ahab! What is it that you want from me?

Have not you rebuked me for not restoring Alcibiades to life?
Saint Paul stepped forward: *enough, creature! Are you angel or demon?*
Burning sage, Paul said: *observe my Jupiter medallion*[194], *be in fear!*

I command you reveal to us your true name: end this charade!
Wily wizard! You ask what is my name? Prepare to quake!
For you have disturbed Mephistopheles, the Prince of Lies!

---

186 Mark Twain, *The Duke And Dauphin, The Adventures of Huckleberry Finn*

187 Gerald Gardner, *Book of Shadows*; Kate Bush, *Waking The Witch*; Myrick And Sánchez, *The Blair Witch Project*

188 William Shakespeare, *King Lear*

189 Rainer Maria Rilke, *Duino Elegies*

190 Yukio Mishima, *Confessions of A Mask*

191 The Bible, *The Acts of The Apostles*

192 Christopher Marlowe, *Doctor Faustus*; Johann Wolfgang van Goethe, *Faust*; The Rider-Waite Tarot Deck, *The Devil*; Lil Nas X, *Montero*

193 Joyce Kilmer, *Trees*

194 Joseph Smith, *American Prophet*

The Rainbow Cantos

Ahab's Poetry III: The Rape of Europa[195]

By Toussaint L'Ouverture[196]

Toussaint: Mademoiselle ~ *may I take you away?*

Europa: Gasp! What is it you intend for me?

Toussaint: *I mean to grant you a better life!*

Europa: Me? To the Europeans I am but *meat*!

Toussaint: *I am here to take you away from all of that!*

Europa: No European cares for me the way you do!

Toussaint: *Let us go, then, you and I*[197] *~ away from here!*

Europa: *Bliss! Bliss!* Such a man of honor and decorum!

Narraror: *Thus transpired the rape of Europa by Toussaint L'Ouverture.*

---

195 Titian, *The Rape of Europa*

196 C.L.R. James, *Toussaint Louverture*

197 T.S. Elliot, *The Love Song of J. Alfred Prufrock*

The Demonic Possession[198] of Ishmael Daedalus

From fairy to demon Mephistopheles morphed into his true form[199]:
seven feet tall, angelic wings, pearly whites galore, and a chiseled physique[200];
tell me children ~ Saint Paul ~ what is it I am going to do with you?

Shall I flay you? Roast you? Which style would you prefer?
No ~ *while fair is foul, and foul is fair*[201] ~ you are special to me ~
and *something wicked this way comes*[202]: Daedalus ~ *a perfect host!*

Mephistopheles vaporized into thin air and made his way to Ishmael:
convulsion[203]! In the not so far away distance was a black crow[204]:
and the crow went: *caw, caw, caw, caw, caw, caw, caw!*

---

198 Charles Baudelaire, *The Possessed*
199 Raphael, *The Transfiguration*
200 William Blake, *Satan In His Original Glory*
201 William Shakespeare, *MacBeth*
202 Ibid
203 William Friedkin, *The Exorcist*
204 Ted Hughes, *Crow*

The Rainbow Cantos

The Withdrawal of Saint Paul

Jesus, Mary, and Joseph[205] – *were but you now here to expel this demon!*
Off to the Alchemist's Guild shall go I – to seek counsel on Mephistopheles:
never before has the devil himself possessed the president of a university!

Hadrian! Antinous! Ahab! Keep tame this beast[206] for the duration of my absence!
Into the night vanished Saint Paul and the children were there left abandoned.
Antinous said: how has Oberon – Mephistopheles – *truly* barbed us?

Are not we *beings-toward-death*[207]? Let us ask of Mephistopheles instead:
where now is Alcibiades – in *heaven with the angels* or in *hell with the demons*?
Ishmael floated up into the sky but called down from above: he burns in hell!

Rendezvous At Antinous's Childhood Treehouse

In safety are we huddled here tonight – far away from Sargasso State and Mephisto!
More than vampires haunt those ancient halls on the banks of the old Raritan –
the very cosmos themselves call out to us: *hurry up – please – it's time*[208]!

Antinous continued: we must assemble a *dossier* on Mephisto: *what is his nature*[209]?
When we knew him as *Oberon*, he was gentle with us – *is he truly an enemy*[210]?
Now that Mephisto controls President Daedalus, *who knows how he will act!*

Will the devil himself be able to withstand the *bureaucracy* of the Presidency?
Perhaps we need do nothing but merely set the deans and frat boys upon him!
In the meantime, we must consult with the *wise* as to how we ought proceed.

---

205 Paul Guaguin, *Geburt Christi, des Gottessohnes*
206 The Bible, Saint John of Patmos, *The Book of Revelation*
207 Martin Heidegger, *Being And Time*
208 T.S. Elliot, *The Wasteland*
209 Lucretius, *On The Nature of Things*
210 Carl Schmitt, *The Concept of the Political*

Prospero Crowley Consulted: Let Us Resort, Then, To Magick!

Beethoven's *Sixth Symphony*[211] played in Professor Crowley's office.
How can I be of service to you three? And my tears for Lolita!
Did a specimen of her caliber need turn to fanaticism and monasticism?

Forget Lolita! Crowley, we come to you with a desperate plea for help!
Read the syllabus! No extra credit shall be doled out, whatsoever!
This is not about extra credit but instead about saving *souls eternal*:

President Ishmael Daedalus is *possessed* by the devil: *we are in danger!*
By the devil, you say? Well *on the side* I am a Yoruba witch doctor –
it helps pay off my mortgage – to rectify this, let us resort, then, to magick!

Lolita Takes Her Vows: Introducing Sister Lola Montez[212]

No longer shall I live a life reigned by foolishness: *I pledge myself to Dionysus*[213]!
Before I was born again, I sinned frivolously: *now must I sin piously!*
What is decadence[214]? What is polyamory? *Teach me what love is, Dionysus!*

Teach me to revere my womanly cycle rather than to find disgust in it!
Let me savor intricate loves rather than furious and destructive ones!
Let me perform the Dionysian rites *nightly, justly, and sanctimoniously!*

Leave me not my name, for I can always take on another in this life[215];
present to me my *thyrsus*[216]: *who now denies that I belong to Dionysus?*
Henceforward shall I be known as Sister Lola Montez: *farewell, Lolita!*

---

211 Ludwig van Beethoven, *The Pastoral Symphony*
212 Eliza Rosanna Gilbert, Countess of Landsfeld
213 Euripides, *The Bacchae*; Giovanni Bellini, *The Infant Bacchus*; Jacob Jordaens, *Bacchus As A Child*
214 Richard Gilman, *Decadence: The Strange Life of An Epithet*
215 Arthur Miller, *The Crucible*
216 Dionysian Ceremonial Rod, Adorned With A Pinecone

The Rainbow Cantos

And Then They Drank From The Cask of Amontillado[217]

Splish, splash went the Italian wine[218] in the glass: *pour me another one!*
Welcome to my chateau ~ *Orisha Haus* ~ hummed Prospero Crowley.
Professor Crowley ~ *teach us your metaphysics*[219] ~ who is Mephisto?

In Yoruba he is referred to as *Eshu* ~ in South America ~ *el Diablo.*
Is he *benefic* or *malefic*? Or is he *capricious* and *mercurial*?
Mischief ~ *whether holy or unholy* ~ is the business of Mephisto!

That is why he fooled us into thinking that he was Lord of the Fae!
Saint Paul of Tarsus told us that he was a demon, *is that true?*
He is more of an *imp* than a *demon*: " Saint " Paul is incorrect.

Mephisto's Presidential Proclamation I: Turn Water Into Wine[220]!

In the beginning there was only water, and the spirit rushed over it[221]:
I award this state of affairs a C + and hereby alter it effective immediately:
instead of serving water at the dining hall, *wine must be served to all.*

Indeed, *every water fountain across the five campuses must now dispense wine;*
in the meantime, I will now have another glass of sauvignon blanc, *s'il vous plaît.*
Any student apprehended drinking water must undergo alcohol education training!

Students have been bringing liquor into their classes since *time immemorial:*
it is time we celebrate their valiant efforts and reward them for their virtue!
At the time of writing this I am *intoxicated* ~ signed President Daedalus.

---

217   Edgar Allen Poe, The Cask of Amontillado
218   Charles Baudelaire, Lovers' Wine
219   Aristotle, The Metaphysics
220   The Bible, The Gospel of Saint John
221   The Book of Genesis

Ahab's Poetry IV: El Diablo On The Runway[223]

El Diablo On The Runway

Yaaas bitch!
Now gyrate[223]!
Gucci glamor!
Move those hips –
shake that ass!
Dior delicious –
absolutely stunning –
keep it going,
werk that body –
drop with the bass –
Louis Vuitton lovely –
Yaaas queen!
Hermès handsome!
You know what?
I'm so shook –
I'm blown away[224]!

---

222 RuPaul's Drag Race
223 W.B. Yeats, The Second Coming
224 Wendy Williams, The Wendy Williams Show

The Rainbow Cantos

Mephisto's Presidential Proclamation II: Victorianism Is Our Cross[225]!

Let soul clap its hands and sing, and louder sing[226]:
as of now Victorianisms[227] are abolished at Sargasso State!
For is not man animal[228]? *Turn now to your instincts[229]!*

Libations are already required: but what ought they yield?
Vivacity! An aged man is but a paltry thing[230]: *live while young!*
What is the state of nature[231]? *Nothing other than pure bliss!*

Any Victorian caught being prudish must go: *expulsion awaits!*
I fear I have worked us all into a passion[232]: *Victorianism is our cross.*
Dionysus teaches: go now, two by two[233], *making love to one another!*

---

225 Giotto di Bondone, Scroveoni Chapel; Raphael, The Mond Crucifixion
226 W.B. Yeats, Sailing To Byzantium
227 Michel Foucault, The History of Sexuality: An Introduction
228 Aristotle, De Anima; Charles Darwin, On the Origin of Species
229 Sigmund Freud, Civilization And Its Discontents
230 W.B. Yeats, Sailing To Byzantium
231 Thomas Hobbes, John Locke, J.J. Rousseau, etc.
232 Jesus Christ's Passion, The New Testament
233 The Bible, The Gospel of Saint Mark, The Gospel of Saint Luke

Sermon[234]: Thus Spoke Chaplain Zarathustra

Is not the moment gorgeous? The young in one another's arms[235]...
how President Daedalus looks after us all! Spoiled are we!
Divine Providence[236] *is with us: Dionysus devours Christological lamb chops*[237]*!*

The *supper of the lamb*[238] *is succulent* indeed: *we are all licking our fingers!*
This is the dawn of a new era for Sargasso State: Daedalus guides us!
What are we called to do? Nothing other than to enjoy life: revel in it all!

To close out my sermon, I must admonish any *puritans* among you:
we are living in a new age[239] *~ one of increased freedom and release ~*
we have nothing to lose but our chains[240]: *and they are self-imposed!*

Mephisto's Presidential Proclamation III: Football Is Sacred[241]!

From this point onward, most of the research funds will go to sports.
Every football game in particular will become *mandatory* for all students:
even the faculty and deans must attend every single football game.

Any nerd or dweeb must apprentice to an athlete, *as would a squire to a knight*[242].
There will now be school uniforms for all faculty, students, and deans:
sports jerseys, beer-can hats, and jogger leggings ~ *for beauteous*[243] *are legs!*

Anyone found in direct violation of these new mandates will be *reprimanded*:
fifty laps around the football stadium while everyone sneers and boos at them!
Go Sargasso State! Go Sargasso Wild Knights! Go football! Play ball!

---

234 Johnathan Edwards, *Sinners In The Hands Of An Angry God*
235 W.B. Yeats, *Sailing To Byzantium*
236 John Calvin, *Institutes Of The Christian Religion*
237 Shari Lewis, *Lamb Chop*
238 The Bible, Saint John of Patmos, *The Book of Revelation*
239 Rado and Ragni, *Aquarius/Let The Sunshine In*
240 Karl Marx, *The Communist Manifesto*
241 William C. Dowling, *Confessions Of A Spoilsport*
242 Chaucer, *The Canterbury Tales*; Lord Byron, *Childe Harold's Pilgrimage*
243 William Wordsworth, *It Is A Beauteous Evening, Calm And Free*

The Rainbow Cantos

Ahab's Poetry V: Poolside Resurrection[244]

Poolside Resurrection

The scene: blue chlorine water,
a prevailing sense of calmness,
no need to worry, swim! *Swim!*
Young, enjoy yourself, *paddle!*
Merry, *making giddy*, happy as
could be, swim free, worry not.

Pardon me: I never said that the
above would last forever, now it
      *is time to gamble: you're about
      to drown! Good luck! Despair*,
hopelessness, darkness, cold,
water entering your two lungs.

      *Ah, the lifeguard: he cannot
      help you now, or can he? Let
      us take bets out on it. Borrowed*
breath enters your lungs, he hits
      *your chest, breathe! Breathe! O,
      so, it looks like you're not dead yet.*

---

244 The Bible, The Gospel of Saint John; Carl Heinrich Bloch, The Raising of Lazarus

Ahab Dreams[245] of The Whale[246]

Fishing boat[247]. Out in the Raritan. No catches all day. *Day becomes night*[248]: cast out your nets one more time – *over yonder should you all do it*[249]. From out the corner south[250] they cast out their nets one more time:

we have caught something – reel in the nets – *let us behold our catch!* The nets will not return? *The catch is too bountiful?* What is it? Now the boat was pulled several yards by the netted creature –

I forgot to pray this morning – *is this my fate* – my swift justice? *It jumped into the air - a white whale - only God can aid us now!* Then the boat capsized, and Ahab was swallowed by the great beast[251]!

---

245 Henry Fuseli, *The Nightmare*; Edgar Allen Poe, *Dream-Land*, *A Dream Within A Dream*; Charles Baudelaire, *Dream of A Curious Person*

246 Herman Melville, *Moby Dick*

247 Charles Baudelaire, *The Splendid Ship*; Arthur Rimbaud, *The Drunken Boat*

248 James Joyce, *Finnegan's Wake*

249 The Bible, *The Gospel of Saint Luke*, *The Gospel of Saint John*

250 Robert Browning, *The Bishop Orders His Tomb At Saint Praxed's Church*

251 The Bible, *The Book of Jonah*

The Rainbow Cantos

Doctor de Sade's Office II: Increase In Xanax

Doctor de Sade in my dream was I eaten by a *gargantuan*[252] *whale!*
My slumber offers me no respite – *I am abandoned to my anxiety!*
Ahab knew he could not tell de Sade that he had staked his mother.

In truth Lilith de Sade still haunted his night tremors every so often.
How many more nights must I go *sleepless*[253] Doctor de Sade? *Tell me!*
Going forward we will increase your xanax to mediate your anxiety.

How goes Lolita, *your friend?* I have not seen her in quite some time.
She goes now by the name of *Sister Lola Montez* and is quite *pious.*
Doctor de Sade wondered if Lolita had perhaps already forgotten him.

The Witch[254] Doctor Is In: I Scry The Leviathan[255]!

Children – who among you can discern the natures of the gods?
Speak up! Or do you admit the fallaciousness of your gods?
Antinous said: *we were all atheists before Mephisto appeared to us!*

Atheists[256]? *What manner of folly is this? Do you speak a falsehood?*
We were all members of the Leftist Society – *we worshiped Marx!*
So, you were dialectical materialists, then: *but Yoruba is superior!*

Crowley gazed into the scrying bowl, and something came into vision:
I scry the Leviathan! A giant white whale as big as Columbus Circle[257]!
Just then Ahab fainted: *he would need an increase in Xanax afterwards.*

---

252 François Rabelais, Gargantua And Pantagruel
253 Edgar Allen Poe, The Valley of Unrest
254 Francisco Goya, Witches' Sabbath
255 The Bible, The Book of Isaiah; Thomas Hobbes, The Leviathan
256 Richard Dawkins, The God Delusion
257 New York City

School Newspaper: Wild Knights Have Wild Nights[258]!

Everybody knows that since President Daedalus's *radical* reforms:
the Scarlet Wild Knights have been having *wild nights* partying!
Students pre-game before class and then drink after class, too;

The dorm staffers are not writing up kids for drinking[259] anymore;
Daedalus will soon reform *marijuana* policy, too, an insider said.
A trusted source claims student life is the better for these reforms.

Perhaps attending college is worthwhile *after all*, one student said.
Those who disagree with Daedalus's reforms are clowns *a priori*[260].
In other news, Sargasso State's submarine traversed the ocean blue!

Ahab's Poetry VI: Papa Flee[261]

Papa Flee

Papa is trying to get rid of me:
he never liked a ~ *flea.*
All my flea brothers,
all my flea sisters,
now from Papa Flea:
they flee, flee, hop...
Papa never liked me ~
now I gotta make like a flea:
and flee, flee, hop...
Papa's trying to kill me ~
he doesn't like me one bit...
Papa's trying to poison me ~
he ain't never loved me,
the way Momma Flea did...
Papa already killed Momma,
and she was a fast flea ~
shame he ever caught her at all ~
except ~ *then there never woulda been me.*

---

258 Emily Dickinson, *Wild Nights - Wild Nights!*

259 Pabst Blue Ribbon

260 Immanuel Kant, *Logic*

261 Sylvia Plath, *Daddy*; Kathy Acker, *Hannibal Lecter, My Father*

The Rainbow Cantos

And Thus, The Heart Will Break, Yet Brokenly Live On[262]

Alcibiades's birthday[263] came around and Ahab fell to his knees:
naked I came from my mother's womb, and naked shall I return[264]!
Off to the ground fell his clothes and into the Raritan he swam:

I shall drown in this river just as I have drowned in the pool of love!
Cupid[265]? What about him? The villain! He has waterboarded me!
I curse Aphrodite[266]! Damn her and her happy-go-lucky acolytes!

From the shore Antinous and Hadrian halted their coitus: Ahab!
Swim back to us? Ahab! He did not listen... so Hadrian did this:
like Charon[267] he paddled a boat out to Ahab and scooped him up.

Pride and Prejudice and Poppers[268]

It is a truth universally acknowledged ~ Hadrian attend to my words ~
that a single man in possession of a good fortune, *must be in want of a husband*[269]!
We are but young and in love, but I feel as though you have always been mine:

tell me, will you be more than just my lover? My heartbeat resounds:
bump bump! bump bump! In ecstasy, it goes: *bump bump! bump bump!*
Where did you buy these poppers, that get me going so wildly, Hadrian?

However good as these poppers may be ~ *it is because of you that my heart races!*
Oh Antinous, your sweetness knows no bounds ~ *how could I not love you?*
How could we not become the I that is we, the we that is I[270]? A Dionysian service it is!

---

262   Lord Byron, *Childe Harold's Pilgrimage*
263   Ted Hughes, *Birthday Letters*
264   The Bible, *The Book of Job*
265   Adolf Ulrik Wertmüller, *Cupid As Bacchus*
266   Adolph Hirémy-Hirschl, *The Birth of Venus*
267   Charles Baudelaire, *Don Juan In Hell*
268   Jane Austen, *Pride and Prejudice*
269   Ibid
270   G.W.F. Hegel, *Phenomenology of Mind*

# Kiss Me, Ahab!

Ahab's Poetry VII: Crystalline Ballet Dancers, Three[271]

Crystalline Ballet Dancers, Three

Crystalline ballet
dancers: *three*;
plus you & me;
I love you... so
why did you take
a *hammer*... to our
crystalline ballet
dancers, *three*?
Because... *obviously*,
you loved me...?

Mephisto and Screwtape[272] Sit For High Tea

Indeed, the safest road to hell is the gradual one[273]... *but you know this...*
Oh Mephisto ~ my old friend ~ how much evil you have wrought up here!
Ah Screwtape ~ you know that the thief comes not but to *steal, kill, and destroy*[274]!

Aye! Our mantra: farewell remorse; all good to us is lost ~ *evil be thou our good*[275]!
Screwtape ~ pass me a cucumber sandwich[276] ~ *how goes hell without little old me?*
Papa Legba[277] stewards with a firm hand ~ Virgil still gives tours[278] ~ Charon still boats[279].

Excellent: for, I may elect to stay here a while: my regards to Papa Legba, et cetera!
And what will you have us do to Asmodeus? He murdered your favorite!
True ~ he did slay my Alcibiades ~ yet now Alcibiades is mine forever in hell!

---

271 Edgar Degas, The Dance Foyer At The Opera On The Rue Le Peletier
272 C.S. Lewis, The Screwtape Letters
273 Ibid
274 The Bible, The Gospel of Saint John
275 John Milton, Paradise Lost
276 Oscar Wilde, The Importance of Being Earnest
277 Holly Sierra, Papa Legba - Spirit Guide For The Voodoo Religion
278 Dante Alighieri, The Inferno
279 Luca Giordano, Charon

The Rainbow Cantos

Ahab's Poetry VIII: Fitzpatrick The Fetus Aborts Mommie Dearest[280]

Fitzpatrick The Fetus Aborts Mommie Dearest

It was the eve of the third trimester,
and his whole world was amiss:

inside her belly he kicked then wailed,
triggered: *I can no longer handle this!*

She is in your hands, doctor: *can
you do me this treasonous deed?*

It shall be done, wild young man:
I promise you she shall not bleed.

His mother was cut off around him,
and then became an item of the past...

*Happily, he sobbed: free at last!
Thank God almighty, I am free at last*[281]*!*

---

280 Frank Perry, *Mommie Dearest*

281 The Reverend Doctor Martin Luther King, Jr., *I Have A Dream*

Sister Montez Ministers To The Nerdy

Nerds! Come hither! Attend to my words: who among you knows how to party?
Not us, Sister Montez! We are nerds through and through: have mercy upon us!
Fret not! My lord god Dionysus does not discriminate: all are welcome at his banquet table!

Let me tell you a story: once there was a dweeb *so* incompetent, he *never* learned to party!
For forty days and forty nights[282] he prayed to Dionysus: *finally, were his prayers answered*:
oh lord god – *even though I study Computer Science* – may I please find a girlfriend!

Dionysus said to him: *very well* – this will I grant to you – *if you offer me some Hennessey.*
Do you not see, *nerds*, how Dionysus's loving hand extends out to all, *even to dweebs*?
Yes, Sister Montez! How you have changed our lives! Raise your glasses! Hail Dionysus!

---

282   The Bible, The Book of Genesis, The Gospel of Saint Matthew, The Gospel of Saint Mark, The Gospel of Saint Luke

Ahab's Poetry IX: Miss Betsy On Her Bench

Birds flew by, Miss Betsy on her
bench, looking at all the flowers[283]
opposite her in the park grove -
men and women walked by her -
all saw Miss Betsy there in peace,
    but her Mona Lisa[284] face - bland,
    expressionless - hinted not at her
true reality: *inner oceans of pain,*
entire universes full of hatred; no,
none could see young Bess as a pot
in which volcanoes full of fire and
passion brewed, none saw her as
the nonchalant *mass murderer* she
could be on the inside, *all must go,*
she repeated - *all must die* - she felt,
her life force one and the same with
a drive to *punish, obliterate,* even
to *destroy with impunity*, all power
at her feet, *her majesty Miss Betsy,*
who was never suspected for all
her *queer motives*, underneath the
waves and smiles she doles out to
the *despicables* on a daily basis; no,
none saw her rage coming, and,
that is how she engulfed them in her
eruption[285]: now she is the only entity
in existence, a mountain[286] returned to
her original *virtue* or *sin* of silence

---

283 Claude Monet, *Waterlilies*

284 Leonardo da Vinci, *Mona Lisa*

285 Jacob More, *Mount Vesuvius In Eruption*

286 The Bible, *The Book of Exodus*; Thomas Merton, *The Seven Storey Mountain*; James Baldwin, *Go Tell It On The Mountain*

A Matrimony Uninterrupted: Bells! Bells! Bells![287]

When you, Antinous, look me in the eyes - I know you to be sincere!
When you, Hadrian, take me by the hand - I know our love is strong!
Today is our special day: off we go to be wed by Chaplain Zarathustra!

Hold me in your arms forever ~ for I am too weak to stand by myself!
Then Antinous said: *Hadrian ~ I will never let go of you... forever and ever!*
Ahab could not stomach another wedding so soon after his own...

Chaplain Zarathustra asked them for the necessary words: *I do! I do!*
From his office Mephisto teared up: *they may as well be my own children!*
Only this lay in their future: *more happy love! More happy, happy love!*[288]

---

287 Edgar Allen Poe, *The Bells*; Richard Wagner, *Bridal Chorus*
288 John Keats, *Ode To A Grecian Urn*

The Rainbow Cantos

Omen[289]: Lightning Strikes At The Ginkgo Tree

We are gathered here today as part of a memorial[290] service for Alcibiades:
Chaplain Zarathustra then anointed the Ginkgo tree with essential oils.
Alcibiades wore patchouli - a scent both hated and beloved - like himself.

In the distance birds began to scatter - as if chased by Wagnerian valkyries[291].
A crow landed on a branch of the Ginkgo tree and ceased not to caw...
From the Raritan came gusts of wind so severe that the Ginkgo shook.

Antinous said: look, a storm is brewing: double, double, toil and trouble[292]!
Thunder bellowed in the air and then the sky itself teared for dear Alcibiades.
A message from the grave: lightning struck the Ginkgo tree and lit it aflame[293]!

The Exorcism Of Ishmael Daedalus

For an awards ceremony was the group invited to Mephisto's presidential mansion[294]:
congratulations on your marriage, Antinous and Hadrian: cheers to you both!
The friend circle had come around to Mephisto: he just had so much swagger.

Why on earth did you mount a Gauguin[295] painting on the wall, Mephisto?
Because he is an absolutely corrupted and vile artist - how unvirtuous is he!
There was a commotion at the front door: Mephisto said: no nerds allowed!

An explosion was heard: suddenly Saint Paul entered the room: I am returned
more powerful than ever[296]: prudery shall triumph: demon I cast you out[297]!
Ishmael Daedalus contorted, then Mephisto left him and pranced back to hell.

---

289 Richard Donner, The Omen
290 Alfred Lord Tennyson, In Memoriam A. H. H.
291 Richard Wagner, The Ring Cycle
292 William Shakespeare, MacBeth
293 The Bible, The Book of Exodus
294 Ben Johnson, To Penshurst
295 Paul Guaguin, French Artist
296 J.R.R. Tolkien, The Lord of The Rings: The Two Towers
297 William Friedkin, The Exorcist

Alcibiades In Hell[298]

We have all seen him ~ *in the pantomime* ~ sent to the devil somewhat before his time[299]:
Alcibiades in hell: adjacent Mephisto, Papa Legba, Belial[300], Degas[301], and Lord Byron.
Shall we play another game of palace? Or bridge? Butler ~ *pour more absinthe*[302]!

    How hell is a magickal place! Did you not - Mephisto - make Sargasso a hell on earth?
    Indeed, during my tenure as president I accomplished many precocious reforms!
    But before I could mandate marijuana use for all students, " Saint " Paul intervened...

    What a sorry old prude, said Alcibiades; but at least you are in hell with me again!
    Tell me: what gives " Saint " Paul his powers? How can he expel a demonic prince?
Oh ~ that is a joke we play with the exorcists ~ we let them *think* they have power over us!

---

298 Charles Baudelaire, *Don Juan In Hell*

299 Lord Byron, *Don Juan*

300 Ars Goetia

301 Edgar Degas, Artist

302 Edouard Manet, *The Absinthe DRINKER*; Edgar Degas, *The Absinthe Drinkers In A Cafe*; Pablo Picasso, *The Absinthe Drinker*

The Rainbow Cantos

Division III: Innocence Regained[303]

---

[303] John Milton, *Paradise Regained*

The Rainbow Cantos

Where Were You On The Ides Of March[304], Two Thousand Twenty-One?

Try to remember: where were you on the Ides of March, two thousand twenty-one?
I do not remember - that was many years ago - *who are you? - what do you want?*
I am the granddaughter of Antinous and Hadrian - they told me everything about you.

I never saw them again after that night. Mephisto was one thing - but a living god?
And what did that living god do to you, Ahab, *help me to understand...*
It is none of your business - *I never told anyone of that night* - not even my partners!

Look around you, Ahab, we are in a nursing home - what do you stand to lose?
Everything! What happened to me was special: it belongs to me and me alone:
how would you feel - if the living god *Dionysus* appeared - *and kissed you on the lips?*

[304] William Shakespeare, *Julius Caesar*

In Search of Lost Time: A Madeleine For Ahab[305]

What was the name of Antinous and Hadrian's progeny again? *Ah yes:*
her name was Mrs. Clarissa Dalloway - *what a probing woman she was!*
At least she left for me a fine snack: *a French madeleine*, to dip into my tea...

As he tasted the madeleine it all came back to him: his times at Sargasso State!
What is this newfound burden: have I not enough to bear in my old age[306]?
Lolita. Lilith. Prospero. Trimalchio. Saint Paul. Mephisto. Dionysus...

What times we enjoyed on the banks of the old Raritan: *how young we all were!*
And now Dalloway comes to hear my story... *does she know of the whale?*
What of my old friends? Are they living or are they dead? What of Alcibiades?

Clarissa's Poetry I: Jesus In The Bathtub[307]

Jesus In the Bathtub

A glow fills the room:
Mary pours warm water
into the basin beside the
smiling face of baby[308] Jesus -
whose eyes meet hers -
as she scoops him up
into her arms for a hug,
before lowering him into
the sudsy pool of bubbles
for one of his regular baths[309]...

---

305 Marcel Proust, *In Search of Lost Time*
306 Maya Angelou, *On Aging*
307 Leonardo da Vinci, *The Virgin of The Rocks*
308 Vincent van Gogh, *Madame Roulin And Her Baby*
309 Jacques-Louis David, *The Death of Marat*

The Rainbow Cantos

Mrs. Dalloway[310] Snubs The Emperor of Ice Cream[311]

Twins! Viola and Sebastian[312], come to your mother: lunch awaits at home!
How was preschool today? Shall we sing *Baby Shark* again? One. Two. Three...
Clarissa Dalloway was a careful driver on the road: she loved her children too much.

Viola and Sebastian[313] were two *frisky* Virgo children always scheming after something...
Mommie! We can hear the ice cream truck siren - how we both crave an ice cream pop!
What did I tell you about high fructose corn syrup? We have organic pops at home...

Mommie! Show and tell is right around the corner: what shall we bring to show?
Viola, you bring your *chess trophy* and Sebastian you bring your copy of *Brideshead Revisited*[314].
Sebastian *bemoaned*: I would rather bring in my copy of William Shakespeare's *Twelfth Night!*

---

310 Virginia Woolf, Mrs. Dalloway
311 Wallace Stevens, The Emperor of Ice Cream
312 William Shakespeare, The Twelfth Night
313 El Greco, Saint Sebastian; Owe Zeroe, Saint Sebastian
314 Evelyn Waugh, Brideshead Revisited

Clarissa's Poetry II: Berries For Dessert[315]

Berries For Dessert

A carton of blackberries
carried in by the head chef
sits shining on the countertop:
silence surrounds the berries.
For dessert – *berries and cream*;
nature birthes berries blindly –
but meticulous is the chef.

Naked before the head chef:
berries are weighed by the man –
as Osiris[316] might weigh hearts,
outside the gates of Heaven;
rotten berries do not pass
the selection of the chef –
some berries are in the elect[317].

Berries in the dessert bowl
are *donned* with sugar and cream:
although none of them *deserved*
their gifted *accidental favor* –
granted by the head chef;
nevertheless are they *blessed*,
while some are less fortunate.

---

315 SYLVIA PLATH, BLACKBERRYING; MARGARET ATWOOD, BLACKBERRIES
316 OSIRIS, THE OXFORD ENCYCLOPEDIA OF ANCIENT EGYPT
317 JOHN CALVIN, INSTITUTES OF THE CHRISTIAN RELIGION

Nursing Home Recreation I: Mercutio[318] The Fool

Allo! I am Mercutio the Fool! I am here to entertain you, Mister Ahab!
A fool? In a nursing home? O, let me not be mad - not mad - sweet heaven[319]!
Do you know the difference, old man, between a *sweet fool* and a *bitter fool*[320]?

You cannot fool me, Mercutio - clearly, I am gone soft in the head: woe is me!
No! my job is not to cause strife, but to crank open high windows[321] of fresh air!
Crank, indeed! That is what you are, but I - what am I? I shall tell you:

I am but a poor, infirm, weak, and despised old man[322] ~ I arrive at my destiny:
to be lulled into a false sense of security by a cheaply hired nursing home gimmick!
Mercutio smiled: cheap? No sir! For, your health insurance pays top dollar!

---

318 WILLIAM SHAKESPEARE, ROMEO AND JULIET
319 WILLIAM SHAKESPEARE, KING LEAR
320 IBID
321 PHILIP LARKIN, HIGH WINDOWS
322 WILLIAM SHAKESPEARE, KING LEAR

Flowers of Evil[323] For A Lachrymose[324] Ahab

Mister Candomblé - that friendly woman Clarissa Dalloway left roses[325] for you today!
Flowers you say? Friendly woman? I confess[326] to you: those are the flowers of evil!
Do you know the last time I experienced even an ounce of human kindness, nurse[327]?

No need to get crotchety, Mister Candomblé: *I think I will take my leave of you, now.*
Humbug[328]! *Curse these flowers! Curse Mercutio!* And curse that woman: *she can go to hell!*
Hell - oh! - my heart longs for the place: to rejoin my friends of old: *to rejoin Alcibiades!*

How can Clarissa know that she affects me, so? Every gift she brings, brings memories!
This suffering is too much for me - nurse - my leg, my leg: I need more morphine[329]!
What *bedamned* gifts will she bring me next? Nabokov's *Lolita*? Plato's *Symposium*? Bah!

---

323 Charles Baudelaire, The Flowers of Evil
324 Wolfgang Amadeus Mozart, Requiem
325 Robert Burns, A Red, Red Rose; John William Waterhouse, Gather Ye Rosebuds While Ye May
326 Charles Baudelaire, The Confession
327 One Flew Over The Cuckoo's Nest: Nurse Ratched
328 Charles Dickens, A Christmas Carol
329 Thomas de Quincey, Confessions of An English Opium-Eater; Aleister Crowley, Diary of A Drug Fiend; Avital Ronell, Crack Wars

The Rainbow Cantos

Clarissa's Poetry III: Childbirth

Childbirth

No, we don't need a condom.

We'll call him Oedipus[330].

It's all numb to me!

You know what my body wants...

Oedipus came out!

I'm on birth control, *don't worry*...

I'm expecting in two weeks.

We need to get him out of there, now!

Looks just like his grandfather!

Push, push, Juliet[331]!

You're too young to be a mother...

That was great sex!

My water broke.

Happy Second Birthday, Oedipus!

This hurts.

Sperm meets egg.

Should I get an abortion, Romeo?

Slide down the birth canal, now...

I threw up this morning.

Want to come back to my place?

---

330 Sophocles, *Oedipus Rex*

331 William Shakespeare, *Romeo And Juliet*; Charles Gounod, *Roméo et Juliette*; Sergei Prokofiev, *Romeo and Juliet*

Lolita's Archived Journal I: The Fetus That Broke The Camel's Back

Ahab! My bounty is as boundless as the sea, my love as deep[332]: ours is a forever love!
Did my heart love till now?... For I never saw true beauty until this very night[333]...
A thing of beauty is a joy forever: its loveliness increases; it will never pass into the void[334]!

What did Aristotle say? That love is composed of a single soul inhabiting two bodies?
But I am not so naive: we are but young lovers in a world full of malice and of depravity!
What did Nietzsche say? There are no beautiful surfaces without terrible depths...

Whom shall we trust? Keats the cuck or Nietzsche the syphilitic madman?
And yet, one must have chaos in one, in order to give birth to a dancing star[335]...
Ahab does not know it... but we have already lost a child: and he will never know it!

---

332   William Shakespeare, Romeo And Juliet
333   Ibid
334   John Keats, Endymion
335   Friedrich Nietzsche

The Rainbow Cantos

Ahab Takes Up An Old Folio Containing Moby Dick[336]

Once ~ if I remember well ~ my life was a feast where all hearts opened, and all wines flowed[337]...
Saint Augustine heard a voice in his garden: *one day so did I*: it said: *take up and read*[338]!
Nurse, fetch for me if you would a book from the library: *any book will sate my thirst*!

What book did you procure for me, nurse? Well go on, then: tell me and *spill your beans*[339]!
Ahab 's heart palpitated as soon as he witnessed the cover: this was not the book I wanted!
Damn Melville! Damn my life! Damn the whale! But: there can be no peace for the wicked[340]...

" *I have seen fermenting marshes like enormous nets, wherein the reeds a Leviathan decays*[341]! "
Was Rimbaud writing about the greatest fiend that I have ever known? And my mother...
Lucretia did nothing to stop it: *it went on for years*... and papa was long gone by that point...

Clarissa's Poetry IV: My Real Friends

My Real Friends

In times like these ~ *consistently* ~
a cigarette will be my friend, but,
would you? I went to the bar for
a drink or two last night, *yummy*:
  alcohol will be my friend, but will
  you? If I join the military, I'll have
  a band of brothers, but would you
  be my sibling? Do you even know
  my name? They know my name ~
over at the convenience store ~ but
I'm not sure you care about me that
much, *do you?* I am not a person,
  I am a thing to you ~ that you walk
  by on occasion ~ I am in your view ~
a part of your landscape ~ but if you
would be my friend, maybe I would
not need to have so many friends,
who hurt me by accident ~ but you ~
you hurt me on purpose ~ you like
to do it ~ *don't you? Please stop!*

---

336 John Keats, On First Looking Into Chapman's Homer
337 Arthur Rimbaud, A Season In Hell
338 Saint Augustine, The Confessions
339 Robert Eggers, The Lighthouse
340 The Bible, The Book of Isaiah
341 Arthur Rimbaud, The Drunken Boat

Lucretia Candomble's Archived Journal I: I Will Say This Predator's Name!

My son Ahab was such a beautiful boy... his kindergarten drawings looked like Chagall's[342] paintings! Where did I go wrong? Was I worse than Madame Rimbaud? My child never deserved any of this... He was so innocent - so brilliant - so bold... perhaps that is what attracted the beast to him?

How I am Grendel's[343] mother! My son is tainted now - how can I still love him after what happened? The monster came up out of the abyss - none of the Orishas told me... they abandoned my family! Perhaps if I had not chased away Ahab's father, the evil eye would never have set its gaze upon us...

A. Dworkin: a man who sticks his cock in a child's mouth belongs to Himmler's circle of hell[344]! All of the women and children who have been abused... where were the gods as each monster razed? I will say this predator's name: it is Cardinal Richelieu[345] Whalepond... damn him to eternal suffering!

---

342   Marc Chagall, French Artist

343   Beowulf; Toni Morrison, The Source of Self-Regard

344   Andrea Dworkin, Feminist Par Excellence

345   Alexandre Dumas, The Three Musketeers

The Rainbow Cantos

Ahab Uses A Walker To Have Reveries Of A Solitary Walker[346]

Nurse ~ *supported by this walker* ~ I am fine by myself: go and mingle with the other nurses...
I am an old man taking a walk in the garden: everything here but me is lush and vivacious!
Old men are so respectable that they are fit to be boiled, said Rimbaud[347]. Was he wrong?

Yes ~ *he was wrong* ~ and an upstart *punk little bastard* too, with only a *modicum* of talent!
Meanwhile the wild geese, high in the clear blue air, are heading home again[348]... *my home...*
My old friends... I am a hundred times happier in my solitude than I would be among them[349]...

Enough musing! Here is the punishment: *forward march*[350]! The nurse approached:
Mister Candomblé, be a good sport and come take your medicine ~ *I have news for you:*
for your limited energy, strength, and resolve: *the doctor prescribes you Adderall!*

Clarissa's Poetry V: No Xanax For Cicadas

No Xanax For Cicadas

In the Garden of Eden[351], one day,
a single apple fell off the *Tree of*
the Knowledge of Good and Evil;
on the grass, a few bugs took to
it, *hungry for a late lunch*; the
worm who took the first little
bite, fled underground; the
spider who tried a bit, let out a
scream so loud, that it lost its
voice; the cicada who gave it a
nibble ~ *just to try it out* ~ got so
overwhelmed with anxiety,
that it *fiddled* its wings together,
in a release of stress: *for it had*
no means to acquire Xanax.

---

346   J.J. Rousseau, *Reveries of A Solitary Walker*
347   Arthur Rimbaud, *A Season In Hell*
348   Mary Oliver, *Wild Geese*
349   J.J. Rousseau, *Reveries of A Solitary Walker*
350   Arthur Rimbaud, *A Season In Hell*
351   The Bible, *The Book of Genesis*

Prune Juice For Ahab Candomblé

The nurse rang a bell: Mister Candomblé - *wake up* - I have your prune juice, *here!*
Away with your prune juice - bring me *forbidden fruit*[352] juice - *that better suits my needs!*
It will allow me to discern: what is good and what is evil: *has my whole life been a failure?*

Let wise Adam and wise Eve be my tutors! They shall teach me how to judge! To know!
To be - or not to be - that is the question[353]: *trouble not my bowels with your prune juice!*
Tell me nurse: what lies at the end of my *awful rowing toward God*[354]? Cinnamon buns?

No! I know my destination: *it is hell* - but this nursing home, too, *is a kind of hell...*[355]
No! In my hell will I be young again, with my old friends, sat opposite Mephisto:
or has he *forgotten* me? For seventy years now my Alcibiades has been dead..

Visit From Clarissa Dalloway I: That Kiss, A Thousand Times Accursed[356]!

Tell me more about the night Dionysus appeared to you all: what was his semblance?
He seemed like a stripling in the first flush of manhood: his rich, dark hair waving about him[357]:
on his strong shoulders he wore a purple robe[358]: he was the picture of health: *the font of all life*[359]...

How intriguing! What kind of ritual were you all performing on that mystical March night?
It was a *routine* bacchanal[360]: we *prayed* and *danced* for bounty in all walks of our lives...
Dionysus - *son of the virgin* - brought the counterpart of bread: *wine, and life's flowing juices*[361].

His blood - *the blood of the grape* - lightened the burden of our mortal misery[362]: *he was our panacea...*
Then why are you so bothered by what transpired on that night, Ahab? *You can tell me...*
Ahab coughed up blood: *and that poison - that kiss - a thousand times accursed!* Alcibiades...

---

352 The Bible, The Book of Genesis; John Milton, Paradise Lost
353 William Shakespeare, Hamlet
354 Anne Sexton, The Awful Rowing Toward God
355 Maya Angelou, I Know Why The Caged Bird Sings
356 Arthur Rimbaud, A Season In Hell
357 Ancient Greek Dionysian Myth
358 Ibid
359 The Bible, The Gospel of Saint John
360 Titian, The Bacchanal of The Andrians
361 Euripides
362 Ibid

The Rainbow Cantos

Clarissa's Poetry VI: Five Hundred Gallons of Scotch Whiskey[363]

Five Hundred Gallons of Scotch Whiskey

Research has shown
that a healthy,
balanced breakfast ~
consists of
five hundred gallons
of scotch whiskey ~
in one's coffee
every morning.
This message has been
brought to you by
a drunken poet...
The research was funded by
a major liquor company.

Ahab Takes A Tumble Amidst The Ginkgo Trees

*Under the shade of the Ginkgo trees Ahab enjoyed a stroll out in the courtyard:
suddenly ~ just as did fall that meteor that slew all the dinosaurs prehistoric ~
Ahab took a tumble ~ and rolled ~ far out of reach from his trusted walker ~*

*Nurse! Nurse! He cried, to no avail: they cannot hear you, he thought...
Then his mind wandered: like Napoleon[364] I have fallen: have I met my Waterloo?
When I have fears that I may cease to be[365]... what may I do to console myself?*

*Behold the child among his newborn blisses[366]... all that is begotten must die...[367]
May I not die a fool! May I not die an Ozymandias[368], whose vainglory embarrasses!
When the spade sinks into gravely ground[369]: who will attend this hermit's[370] funeral?*

---

363 Edgar Allen Poe, Lines On Ale; Emily Dickinson, I Taste A Liquor Never Brewed

364 Paul Hippolyte Delaroche, Napoleon at Fontainebleau, 31 March 1814

365 John Keats, When I Have Fears That I May Cease To Be

366 William Wordsworth, Ode: Intimations of Mortality

367 The Bible, The Gospel of Saint John

368 Percy Bysshe Shelley, Ozymandias

369 Seamus Heaney, Digging

370 The Rider-Waite Tarot Deck, The Hermit

Alcibiades's Archived Journal I: The Grave Is A Fine And Private Place[371]

Had we but world enough ~ *and time* ~ this coyness, Ahab, *would be no crime*[372]:
but at my back I always hear, Time's wingèd chariot hurrying near[373]... *Moreover,*
the grave is a fine and private place, but none ~ I think ~ *do there embrace*[374]...

Now ~ therefore ~ *while the youthful hue sits on your skin like the morning dew*[375]...
if my love is reciprocated... let us share with one another the *tenderest* of affections, for:
beauty is truth, truth beauty: that is all you know on earth, *and all you need to know*[376]!

Being around you melts my *frigid* heart ~ *my past matters not to you* ~ you accept me!
Best roommate I could ever have wished for: *share more with me than merely a bunk bed!*
Let me now gather Antinous and Lolita ~ and take my *plight* to Oberon, Lord of the Fae!

Clarissa's Poetry VII: Caffeine Spinal Tap

Caffeine Spinal Tap

Rise and shine! A big
day: a run through
Central Park, a board
of trustees meeting for
the MOMA[377], and later
plastic surgery with Dr.
Cohen, but not before
a sacred morning ritual:
the caffeine spinal tap!

---

371 Andrew Marvell, *To His Coy Mistress*
372 Ibid
373 Ibid
374 Ibid
375 Ibid
376 John Keats, *Ode To A Grecian Urn*
377 Museum of Modern Art, New York City

The Rainbow Cantos

Lolita's Archived Journal II: I Hear America Singing[378]!

Has anyone supposed it lucky to be born...? *It is just as lucky to die, and I know it*[379]...
I had a vision: *I saw a sleeping babe nestling the breast of its mother*[380]... oh Ahab!
But what did I hear? *I heard America singing!* That was to be my daughter's name: *America!*

Dearest Ahab, this *clandestine miscarriage* has wounded me in ways I shall never be able to relay...
Childhood sweetheart ~ *my first lover!* ~ our love grows stillborn: *I cannot tune out the singing!*
In my dreams my daughter America sings in a choir: *what songs will she never grow up to sing?*

Were she not stolen from us, *I would have given my daughter the world and its pearls*[381]!
It is what it is... says the fool... how will I ever forgive my body for what it has *wrought?*
Once, your image ~ *Ahab* ~ took me to the heights of love ~ *now it only reminds me of her...*

Visit From Clarissa Dalloway II: The Gates Of Hell Are Open Night And Day[382]

Ah, Clarissa, *back again*, are you? To torment me more exquisitely? *Let me die!*
Ahab ~ the gates of hell are open night and day: *smooth is the descent, and easy is the way*[383]:
but to return and view the cheerful skies: *in this the task and mighty labor lies*[384]!

Aye, hell is easy to get to ~ *and a wondrous time I am sure* ~ but I am weak and conflicted!
I have lived to the ripe age of ninety-five, who is to say *what* awaits the dead, and *why?*
I am a pagan, Ahab: *tell me*, what are your religious *convictions* since that day long ago?

Surely after all that has happened in your life, you cannot *merely* be one of those agnostics?
I have met the devil and I have kissed Dionysus: no, I am not one of those *asinine* agnostics ~
but who is to say that the *devil* and *Dionysus* are not one and the same being? *What of that?*

---

378 Walt Whitman, *I Hear America Singing*

379 Walt Whitman, *Leaves of Grass*

380 Walt Whitman, *Mother And Babe*

381 Johannes Vermeer, *Girl With A Pearl Earring*

382 Virgil, *The Aeneid*

383 Ibid

384 Ibid

Clarissa's Poetry VIII: My God Pees On Trees

I love to take my God on walks
in the park: you should see the
way he wags his little tail; wow
and the little guy chases birds,
does he ever! Does your God
pee on trees, too? Better that
he did that than pee on people,
or their belongings, like my God
has done; *naughty fella*, that
one, but my God also curls up
with me in bed: *he is so gentle!*
Oops, did I say God? I meant
to say dog! *What a silly mistake!*

Lucretia Candomblé's Archived Journal II: Pack Up The Moon And Dismantle The Sun[385]

Stop all the clocks[386] ~ cut off the telephone[387] ~ *prevent the dog from barking with a juicy bone*[388]...
He was my working week and my Sunday rest: I thought love would last forever: *I was wrong*[389]!
The stars are not wanted now ~ *put out everyone*: pack up the moon[390] and dismantle the sun[391]!

Better that he had *died* than do this to me: whence now will come my grandchildren? *The stork?*
Damn this *Alcibiades* who has corrupted my son: *had only Ahab not been a fool to Lolita!*
I choose rather to *lose a son than to gain one who is a faggot*: let this serve as a warning:

none of my other children will dare to pull such a stunt on my heart: *thus, shall be my fury!*
No, it was not this bimbo - Alcibiades - who ruined my son - it was Cardinal Richelieu Whalepond!
Though my son may be dead to me now - still shall I drive a harpoon into that insipid Cardinal!

---

385 W.H. Auden, *Funeral Blues*
386 Longines Watches
387 Avital Ronell, *The Telephone Book*
388 W.H. Auden, *Funeral Blues*
389 Ibid
390 The Rider-Waite Tarot Deck, *The Moon*
391 W.H. Auden, *Funeral Blues*

The Rainbow Cantos

Clarissa Dalloway Feuds With Headmaster Svengali[392]

Your children are pathetic ~ *and you are not listening, either* ~ great big she-fool that you are[393]!
Sargasso State Preparatory Academy mandates excellence: *and personally? So do I!*
Without me, your children would be the laughing stocks of New England: *I guarantee it!*

You and the monsters ~ Viola and Sebastian ~ are cut from the same cloth: *I always knew it!*
Svengali ~ *what more do you want from them, for they are but children, and bright, too!*
Bright is a word to describe a lightbulb: *But I demand more than that: I crave supernovas!*

Sheep's head[394]! Can you not see how I know the best interests of your ~ my ~ children?
One day you will come and say ~ *I can hear it now* ~ how we should have listened to Svengali[395]!
I have the sight ~ the green thumb ~ and children are but bonsai trees who require clipping!

Clarissa's Poetry IX: The Seatbelt Monster

The Seatbelt Monster

*Can't find
your seatbelt?*
You'll never
guess why, but
there is a seatbelt
*monster ~ who lives
inside of cars ~*
and it loves to
tug at seatbelts:
bringing them
nearer to its *den*
underneath the
*car seats; next
time, if you*
have trouble
finding your buckle:
*you'll know who
is responsible...*

---

392 George du Maurier, *Trilby*; Anthony Harvey, *Svengali*

393 Ibid

394 Ibid

395 Ibid

Alcibiades's Archived Journal II: Dreams of a Life Spent Together

Ahab - my soul is screaming in ecstasy - every fiber of my being is in love with you[396]!
Why should I seek out another? I am the same as he - his essence speaks through me[397]!
Oberon's fairy magick has succeeded! The gay conversion therapy is complete: Ahab is mine!

Ahab - I wait with silent passion - for one gesture, for one glance - from you[398]!
Dreams[399]! Dreams of a life spent together in harmony and bliss: nothing shall impede us!
Our roots are both strong - we shall live long into the future lovingly beside one another!

Ahab - I am ashamed to call this love human... and afraid of the gods to call it divine[400]...
And now we have solidified plans to travel together into paradise: the gay city of Miami!
If he will not ask me to marry him - then, there, shall I propose the question to him!

---

[396] Rumi, *The Essential Rumi*
[397] Ibid
[398] Ibid
[399] Fleetwood Mac, *Dreams*
[400] Rumi, *The Essential Rumi*

The Rainbow Cantos

Visit From Clarissa Dalloway III:

Griefs Are A Joy Long After[401]

Ahab ~ about Dionysus ~ *I am loathe to disturb you* ~ but it is my family's history, too...
Antinous and Hadrian also shied away from this conversation: for what purpose, I know not...
Ahab said: why cover the same ground again? *It goes against my grain to repeat a tale told once*[402]...

You *know* that you have not told me everything that transpired on that night: *why is that?*
Even my griefs are a joy long after because I remember all I wrought and endured... *but I am weak*[403]!
What was so terrible about a kiss coming from *Dionysus?* Was not he your favorite god?

That accursed kiss would have been... speak no more of this bitter tale that wears my heart away[404]!
Ahab, let me probe: how were you feeling that day when Dionysus *kissed you on the lips?*
Not even *Dionysus* could return Alcibiades from the grave: *I preferred Alcibiades to Dionysus!*

---

401 Homer
402 Ibid
403 Ibid
404 Ibid

Clarissa's Poetry X: Spider Real Estate[405]

Spider Real Estate

Would you like
to move into that
corner of the room,
Mister Spider, or,
were you looking
for *something* a bit
smaller? There is
a *car mirror* outside
that you might be
interested in, or
if *that* is not your
scene, there is a
basement that has
just been put on the
market; *the car plot*
would be a middle
class spider's dream
to build a web on;
so, *what will it be?*

Nursing Home Recreation II: Angels In America[406]

In the nursing home's auditorium - *after bingo one Sunday* - a local troupe came in:
Hello there everybody! Today we shall be performing an American classic: *Angels In America*...
Ahab had never heard of the play, and so realized not how much pain viewing it would stir up...

Ahab understood a line all too well: " I do not understand why I am not dead[407]... "
"... when your heart breaks - you should die... " *and yet he lived to be ninety-five years old!*
Ahab heard another line that troubled him: "The Great Question before us is: are we doomed[408]?...
"

" Will the past release us? Can we change? In time? And we desire that change will come[409]... "
Unsurprisingly, Ahab was not the only audience member who *burst* into tears during the play...
Enough is enough: Ahab left the auditorium and *wheeled* out with his bingo winnings!

---

405 George du Maurier, An Incubus; Kathy Acker, The Childhood Life of The Black Tarantula
406 Tony Kushner, Angels In America
407 Ibid
408 Ibid
409 Ibid

The Rainbow Cantos

Visit From Clarissa Dalloway IV: Taste The Life Eternal!

It was a place that was supposed to be sophisticated: *the phonies were coming in the window*[410]!
I went to Sargasso State, too, Ahab: *what about the place did you find to be so offensive?*
Just because somebody is dead - you do not stop liking them - *everybody just moved on*[411]...

Yes - *we have established that you cared deeply for Alcibiades* - truly am I sorry for your loss:
but most people - *if a god took an interest in them* - would have chosen the god over a *memory*.
Are you telling me that my love for him was *trivial*? *That it could have so soon been forgotten*?

Ahab - all I am saying is that - there is a time and a place for love - but it does not involve the dead!
I eventually moved on: but back then I *was not yet ready for what Dionysus whispered to me*:
in my ear he *breathed: journey*[412] *back to Mount Olympus*[413] *with me, and taste the life eternal...*

---

410   J.D. Salinger, The Catcher In The Rye

411   Ibid

412   James Boswell, A Journey To The Western Islands of Scotland

413   James Thornhill, The Gods On Mount Olympus

Clarissa's Poetry XI: A Lost Penny[414]!

A Lost Penny!

Constable, listen to me:
I did not *steal* it, but it is
my life's current *purpose*
to see this penny returned
to its original owner: I
found it on the street ~ I
can't imagine how much
the owner is *traumatized*
over its disappearance;
listen to me ~ I will do
 any and everything it
 takes - to get this penny
back to its owner. *Okay?*

The Rainbow Cantos

Ahab Preemptively Begins His Embalming Process

I am afraid of dying... but how is this life of mine anything but death itself[415]?
If you want to be able to endure life, prepare for death: said Master Freud[416].
Thus, will I prepare for my death – *but have not I been ready for it for seventy years?*

Ahab knew death was coming soon – his *thanatos*[417] behaved wilder than ever before –
this is no time for banal *odes to grecian urns*[418]! – *my death appears in my rear-view mirror:*
how I pray that there will be no further torment such as a reincarnation of the soul!

Whence shall I commend my soul - if I have one at all - after death becomes me?
Shall I bid my soul to the Elysian Fields? Or would my soul find more solace in hell?
Ahab began to rub oil into his skin: *my end is near: hence begins the embalming process!*

Visit From Clarissa Dalloway V: Time Does Not Bring Relief[419]

Time does not bring relief: they have all lied, who told me time would ease me of my pain[420]!
Alcibiades – I miss him in the weeping of the rain: I want him at the shrinking of the tide[421]!
Yours was a true love, Ahab: I know of no greater tragedy than his *untimely*[422] murder...

Thank you: *seventy years later and countless partners past: it is still him that I dream of...*
You cannot know how hard it has been, Clarissa, but I thank you from deep within:
I thank you for your ear[423] and for your compassion: *I am grateful for your visits!*

Antinous and Hadrian must have made for fine grandparents – how lucky were you!
My mother was their offspring - she is one of the most kindhearted women I know!
And what of Lolita? She was a lover of mine once upon a time, too. Dead? Oh..

---

415   Seneca, Roman Philosopher

416   Sigmund Freud, Psychoanalyst

417   Sigmund Freud, *Beyond The Pleasure Principle*

418   John Keats, *Ode To A Grecian Urn*

419   Edna Saint Vincent Millay, *Time Does Not Bring Relief*

420   Ibid

421   Ibid

422   Friedrich Nietzsche, *Untimely Meditations*

423   Vincent van Gogh, *Self-Portrait With Bandaged Ear*

Clarissa's Poetry XII: Two Voluptuous Breasts[424]

Two Voluptuous Breasts

So much depends
upon

two voluptuous
breasts

glazed with rain
water

beside the white
chickens...

Lucretia Candomble's Archived Journal III: Is This A Dagger I See Before Me[425]?

From this jail cell[426] will I recount the narrative *just as it transpired before my eyes*:
Mrs. Smith - the Cardinal will see you shortly - to discuss this vast donation of yours!
Lucretia - I thought - *look like the innocent flower, but be the serpent underneath it*[427]...

Come! You spirits that tend on mortal thoughts: fill me from crown to toe with direst cruelty[428] - make thick my blood - *stop up the access and passage to remorse... let heaven not peep through*[429]! Is this a dagger which I see before me, the handle toward my hand? *Come, let me clutch you*[430]...

This whale has deformed my son, Ahab: if I do not now do this deed, *injustice will reign!* A phone call rang for the secretary, and a smile lit up her face - she said to Lucretia: Mrs. Smith - gather your belongings - for *his holiness* the Cardinal shall see you now!

---

424 William Carlos Williams, *The Red Wheelbarrow*
425 William Shakespeare, *MacBeth*
426 The Reverend Doctor Martin Luther King, Jr., *Letter From Birmingham Jail*
427 William Shakespeare, *MacBeth*
428 Ibid
429 Ibid
430 Ibid

The Rainbow Cantos

Visit From Clarissa Dalloway VI: Do Not Go Gentle Into This Good Night[431]!

Clarissa - tonight my soul passes on into the next world: I am fading away; I can feel it...
Do not go gentle into this good night: old age should burn and rage against the close of the day[432]:
rage ~ Ahab ~ rage, against the dying of the light[433]: rebuke Nyx and her dance of the eternal night!

Tonight ~ Clarissa ~ I have instructed my dutiful nurse to cease my life support and medications ~
I have lived a life replete with pleasures and bounties - perhaps in the next world I shall find peace?
How wonderful is Death[434]! Death and his brother Sleep[435]! Let me soon drink in from the
Lethe[436]...

Clarissa ~ go to the Ginkgo tree at Sargasso State ~ dig underneath the soil there for a treasure[437]:
in a casket beneath the earth, lies a chalice[438] holied by the Lord of Festivity - Dionysus himself!

Oh, Ahab! Do not go gentle into this good night: rage, rage, against the dying of the light[439]!

---

431 Dylan Thomas, *Do Not Go Gentle Into That Good Night!*
432 Ibid
433 Ibid
434 Carlos Schwabe, *Death And The Grave Digger*
435 Percy Bysshe Shelley, *Queen Mab*
436 Charles Baudelaire, *Lethe*
437 Robert Louis Stevenson, *Treasure Island*
438 Frederick Judd Waugh, *The Knight Of The Holy Grail*
439 Dylan Thomas, *Do Not Go Gentle Into That Good Night!*

Clarissa's Poetry XIII: Death of a Cell Phone[440]

The phone died
seven weeks ago:
too soon for the
priest to get to
it in time to give
it its last rites;
the funeral was
not *unusual* and
progressed along
without too much
grief; *cremation*
was the easiest
route: *the ashes*
were placed in a
plot in a cellular
device cemetery.

---

440 Arthur Miller, *Death of a Salesman*

The Rainbow Cantos

Ahab Is Granted A Vision Of Dionysus In Mourning

Dionysus spoke to his attendants: *maenads*[441]! Tonight, shall we have a feast[442] of mourning ~ for an earthly soul *dear to me* despite his mortality: *so honorable, this one*... tonight: replace my *purple robes* with the *black ones* of a mourner: *even finer wines than usual*!

Now will I have occasion to visit Hades and dine in the vault of Erebus: Ahab beckons! Tomorrow shall we descend into hell: bring along a few treats for Cerberus[443] the hound; who stands to fathom what appreciation an immortal may have for a mere work of clay[444]?

This mortal ~ Ahab ~ refused my invitation to house him here on Mount Olympus's peak: *what courage to deject a god*! Tonight, we all garb black for the man: *we shall celebrate him*! So loyal and just a mortal have I never encountered before: *we shall mourn him righteously*!

The Angel Of Death[445] Comes For Ahab Candombie

The stillness in the room, was like the stillness in the air: between the heaves of storm[446]! Because I flagged down Death ~ as if he were a taxi driver ~ he kindly stopped for me[447]; the taxi held but just ourselves ~ and immortality[448]; we slowly drove: *he knew no haste*[449];

we passed the school[450] ~ where children strove at recess ~ *without remorse, happy and gay*[451]! We passed the fields of gazing grain[452] ~ we passed the setting sun; since that day long ago[453] ~ it has been centuries ~ and yet it all feels shorter than the day I first met Alcibiades[454]...

My friends are well ~ *most are in hell* ~ I, like Persephone[455], traverse back and forth: when not settled atop Mount Olympus in the arms of *cherished Dionysus*, in hell ~ alongside Mephisto[456] and Alcibiades ~ I don Hawaiian shirts: *such is the death*!

---

441 John William Godward, *A Priestess Of Bacchus*
442 Giovanni Bellini And Titian, *The Feast Of The Gods*
443 William Blake, *Cerberus'*
444 The Bible, *The Book Of Genesis*
445 Gustave Moreau, *The Park And The Angel Of Death*
446 Emily Dickinson, *Because I Could Not Stop For Death*
447 Ibid
448 T.S. Elliot, *Whispers Of Immortality*
449 Emily Dickinson, *Because I Could Not Stop For Death*
450 Sargasso State Preparatory Academy
451 Emily Dickinson, *Because I Could Not Stop For Death*
452 Vincent van Gogh, *Wheatfields With Crows*
453 Emily Dickinson, *Because I Could Not Stop For Death*
454 Ibid
455 Edna Saint Vincent Millay, *Prayer To Persephone*
456 Eduard von Grützner, *Mephisto*

Gayowulf

An LGBTQ Epic Poem
in Fifty-Four Cantos
inspired by Beowulf

Grendel, Grendel's Mommy and the Kimono Dragon

Book 2: Gayowulf

◇◇◇

97 BOOK I: GRENDEL

- 98 Book I: Section I: Canto I: Birth Of Gayowulf
- 98 Book I: Section I: Canto II: A Kiss To Kill
- 98 Book I: Section I: Canto III: Grendel The Foe
- 99 Book I: Section I: Canto IV: Birth Of Grendel
- 99 Book I: Section I: Canto V: Gayowulf Must Never Love
- 99 Book I: Section I: Canto VI: Grendel Dons A Mask
- 100 Book I: Section II: Canto I: Witches' Brew
- 101 Book I: Section II: Canto II: Face of Gayowulf
- 101 Book I: Section II: Canto III: Lumberjack Gayowulf
- 101 Book I: Section II: Canto IV: Grendel's Self - Portrait
- 102 Book I: Section II: Canto V: Gayowulf Lands In Manhattan
- 102 Book I: Section II: Canto VI: Gayowulf's Quivering Lips
- 103 Book I: Section III: Canto I: Torn Violently Asunder
- 103 Book I: Section III: Canto II: Doe - Eyes Morning After
- 103 Book I: Section III: Canto III: Gayowulf Dresses Grendel
- 104 Book I: Section III: Canto IV: Grendel's Bedtime Soliloquy
- 104 Book I: Section III: Canto V: Grendel's Art Exhibition
- 104 Book I: Section III: Canto VI: Grendel's Broken Arm

106 BOOK II: GRENDEL'S MOMMY

- 108 Book II: Section I: Canto I: Bathroom Nervous Breakdown
- 108 Book II: Section I: Canto II: Grendel's Open Casket Adieu
- 108 Book II: Section I: Canto III: Requiem For Grendel
- 109 Book II: Section I: Canto IV: A Reception Most Inceptive
- 109 Book II: Section I: Canto V: Park Avenue Menagerie
- 109 Book II: Section I: Canto VI: Call Me Mommy
- 110 Book II: Section II: Canto I: Birth Of Grendel's Mommy
- 110 Book II: Section II: Canto II: Dance Of The Nude Occultists
- 111 Book II: Section II: Canto III: Bath Of The High Priestess
- 111 Book II: Section II: Canto IV: Lactations Of Hecate
- 111 Book II: Section II: Canto V: To The Fair Isle Of Mykonos
- 112 Book II: Section II: Canto VI: All Aboard The S. S. Oscar Wilde
- 113 Book II: Section III: Canto I: Gayowulf Has A Night Tremor
- 113 Book II: Section III: Canto II: Mommy's Secret Whispers
- 113 Book II: Section III: Canto III: Gayowulf Has A Panic Attack
- 114 Book II: Section III: Canto IV: Coitus A La Praying Mantis
- 114 Book II: Section III: Canto V: Bibbity Bobbity Boom
- 114 Book II: Section III: Canto VI: Into The Depths Fades Mommy

116 BOOK III: THE KIMONO DRAGON

118	Book III: Section I: Canto I: Fall Of The House Of Gayowulf
118	Book III: Section I: Canto II: Triple Shot Macchiato
118	Book III: Section I: Canto III: Mopey Dopey Milan Overdose
119	Book III: Section I: Canto IV: Aim For The Heart, Wiglaf
119	Book III: Section I: Canto V: Seal Of The Kimono Dragon
119	Book III: Section I: Canto VI: One Last Dragon To Chase
120	Book III: Section II: Canto I: Gayowulf And Wiglaf Arrive In Japan
120	Book III: Section II: Canto II: Ready, Set, Go - Go
120	Book III: Section II: Canto III: Palace Of The Kimono Dragon
121	Book III: Section II: Canto IV: If His Kimono Could Talk
121	Book III: Section II: Canto V: Off Comes The Kimono For Gayowulf
121	Book III: Section II: Canto VI: Flames Of The Kimono Dragon
122	Book III: Section III: Canto I: The Kimono Dragon Serves Hibachi
122	Book III: Section III: Canto II: Intentions Of The Dragon Revealed
122	Book III: Section III: Canto III: A Kimono Worthy Of The Dragon
123	Book III: Section III: Canto IV: Disco Dance Floor of Death
123	Book III: Section III: Canto V: Gayowulf Attempts Cocaine Roulette
123	Book III: Section III: Canto VI: Wiglaf Out - Snorts The Kimono Dragon

95

The Rainbow Cantos

BOOK I: GRENDEL

The Rainbow Cantos

Book I: Section I: Canto I: Birth Of Gayowulf

A dream: a wolf born to a woman on Walpurgisnacht!
We Weird Sisters, unchained and feral:
Freyja boons us with a champion!
To the cauldron now, behold his name:
Gayowulf! What would this hound do for us?
Vanquisher of enemies! Dreadlord of the night!
Gayowulf! We shall watch from afar:
aiding and abetting you in your feats!
Woman - born, with the heart of a wolf,
but with the head of a serpent!
Our twilight champion: an instrument most sharp!

Book I: Section I: Canto II: A Kiss To Kill

Meditate on our common enemy: Grendel!
We Weird Sisters three do commend
our pet Gayowulf toward Grendel!
Prepare the cauldron for a spell:
ensnare now those two young souls!
When their lips kiss, Grendel shall die!
We three sisters dance and tap our feet:
for, though he may know it not,
Gayowulf does our queen mommy's bidding;
we sisters conclude now our weird dance:
hail Gayowulf, Champion of Freyja!

Book I: Section I: Canto III: Grendel The Foe

A vision: Gayowulf in his teens!
Dark child: fulfill your purpose!
Two babes born on the same night:
Gaze into the cauldron: behold Gayowulf!
Behold Grendel! Two star - crossed foes...
What now? Gayowulf wrestles a lion!
He has bested the beast with his bare hands!
With its mane he stitched a cost most fine.
Talented Gayowulf! Valorous in all he does:
with needle and thread, he works miracles!
How Gayowulf shall smite Grendel the foe!

Book I: Section I: Canto IV: Birth Of Grendel

Opalescent blur: a son cradled by his mommy...
Hark you witches to the scrying glass!
Eye our nemesis giving birth:
how she is calm and collected:
her temperament: diamond and steel!
Out came the babe: the nurses wailed!
What is wrong with my son?
Your son is too beautiful, miss!
Grendel: damned by the witches at birth:
they set upon him the curse of beauty!
Grendel: most beautiful but most evil!

Book I: Section I: Canto V: Gayowulf Must Never Love

Vision: a golem with a beating heart!
Gayowulf exists to do our bidding:
he shall slay Grendel and his mommy for us!
Gayowulf appeared in the scrying glass:
handsome, asleep, and lost in a dream...
In a dreamscape Gayowulf floated:
he outstretched his empty arms:
suddenly a man appeared in them!
Then the witches saw him cuddle his pillow:
no! Never! Gayowulf shall never date!
Gayowulf must never love!

Book I: Section I: Canto VI: Grendel Dons A Mask

Vision: a hammer and chisel adjacent marble...
We witches know: beauty is the worst!
Grendel shall suffer greatly - look:
the crystal ball pictured the monster himself:
Grendel stood tall in the mirror:
bang! The mirror shattered!
Henceforward Grendel covered his face:
wherever he went he would wear a mask!
Beauty too great dissolves into ugliness -
Grendel's beauty had to be concealed!
Artwork enabled Grendel to unravel his soul!

The Rainbow Cantos

Book I: Section II: Canto I: Witches' Brew

Vision: the clock strikes midnight!
Witches! The time comes to set our trap:
sprites of the moon join us for a toast!
Into the cauldron went spices and roots:
come, Weird Sisters! Imbibe upon this drink!
As they drank, their spell took hold on the world!
It is time! Gayowulf must begin his journey –
we have spun a web for Grendel and his mommy!
In but a fortnight Gayowulf shall travel West:
such is his fate! Such is the fate of Grendel!
How Gayowulf in Manhattan shall roost!

Book I: Section II: Canto II: Face of Gayowulf

Dust off the crystal ball! Let us spy upon Grendel!
A masked figure, ready as if for a society dance:
Grendel in full splendor, curls adjoining his profile.
From within his studio, he crafted works of great evil:
painted sculptures of beauteous design: too beautiful!
Yet again does Grendel subdue another slab of granite:
heave! Ho! Down slams the stone; Grendel begins:
his chisel carves out a figure from his dreams:
a face with dangerous lips, fecund and kissable.
Look, Weird Sisters, at what Grendel has done:
Grendel has carved out the face of Gayowulf!

Book I: Section II: Canto III: Lumberjack Gayowulf

Dream: a wolf howls in a moonlit metropolis.
Focus the scrying glass upon Gayowulf!
In a woodlandscape Gayowulf chops trees.
He has stopped now: he returns to his hut:
what is that? Ah! Our magick has worked!
Gayowulf opened a sealed letter:
Congratulations! You have been accepted:
the full - tuition scholarship is yours!
Join us in New York at your earliest convenience!
Gayowulf packed his bags and got ready at once:
he would study Fashion Design in New York City!

Book I: Section II: Canto IV: Grendel's Self - Portrait

Vision: a marsh hawk captures its prey.
How could Grendel know of Gayowulf?
Perhaps his mommy knows of our plot!
What is Grendel doing now?
Even as he showers, he wears the mask!
Grendel dries off and returns to his studio -
come, friend, let me show you my work:
oh, my latest sculpture: a self - portrait!
When the friend saw Grendel's handiwork,
he shrieked: a face so beautiful as to be grotesque!
Grendel's art shattered the man's heart!

The Rainbow Cantos

Book I: Section II: Canto V: Gayowulf Lands In Manhattan

Vision: two lovers in an embrace.
We Weird Sisters are in a good mood:
Gayowulf our vassal is en route -
Manhattan bound; he arrives today.
Once he is there, our plan will unfold:
Rugged Gayowulf shall kiss Grendel the foe!
From his plane window Gayowulf could see:
skyscrapers and the Statue of Liberty!
He left his old country behind:
in America he would plant new seeds.
Still, he longed to kiss a lover on the lips!

Book I: Section II: Canto VI: Gayowulf's Quivering Lips

Vision: two lovebirds sitting in a nest.
According to the stars, they will meet today:
let us tune into the crystal ball and see them!
Both are at the Museum of Modern Art:
Gayowulf ambles and Grendel sketches lilies.
Suddenly Gayowulf enters the room Grendel is in!
Watch, witches, as the two draw near!
Grendel spotted Gayowulf, and was shook:
Gayowulf turns to Grendel and cannot look away:
Grendel rises and walks over to Gayowulf:
and loses his focus over Gayowulf's quivering lips!

Book I: Section III: Canto I: Torn Violently Asunder

A vision: lips fully alive with life!
Watch, witches! Gayowulf is spot on:
he has been invited back to Grendel's lair!
Gayowulf tailed Grendel into his apartment:
paintings and sculptures littered the rooms.
Off came their clothes, torn violently asunder!
Grendel held Gayowulf and Gayowulf held Grendel:
look, witches, at what Gayowulf shall do!
Shall he toss or impale Grendel?
How will he enact our revenge? I cannot watch!
What? Gayowulf nibbles at Grendel's neck!

Book I: Section III: Canto II: Doe-Eyes Morning After

Observation: it is in the nature of bubbles to pop!
How can this be, Weird Sisters?
Gayowulf loves rather than loathes Grendel!
Have we misunderstood our divinations?
Clear is the prophecy: Grendel must die!
Rolling over, Gayowulf knocked off Grendel's mask!
Mysterious lover, why do you cover your face?
Grendel shrugged: if you saw it, you would flee from me!
Come here to me, and let me see ~
uncovering his face Grendel was revealed:
superlative beauty: doe - eyed Gayowulf fawned!

Book I: Section III: Canto III: Gayowulf Dresses Grendel

Vision: barbaric appropriations of black velvet!
Witches! So long as those two shall kiss,
the doom and demise of Grendel is guaranteed!
Let the two therefore dally and play, for:
does not the cat, too, play with its prey?
Today is Gayowulf's first student fashion show!
Immaculate Grendel, will you model for me?
So Gayowulf dressed Grendel from head to toe.
Your designs belong to the night, said Grendel;
I gaze into your eyes and feel a raw emotion:
Grendel continued: *you and I belong together!*

The Rainbow Cantos

Book I: Section III: Canto IV: Grendel's Bedtime Soliloquy

Premonition: a lost and weeping beauty.
Grendel thought: when has beauty ever done any good?
To be beautiful in the world is to be one of the damned!
Hidden have I, all of my life, my monstrous beauty:
yet Gayowulf has not once flinched at my face!
Grendel gazed at the freshly asleep Gayowulf:
be mine, fated lover! But who are you, Gayowulf?
Cherished one, whom I first met in my dreams:
what is it that the stars themselves intend for us?
That is enough for now - off to bed I go!
A nightmare awoke Grendel: he dreamed of bruised lips!

Book I: Section III: Canto V: Grendel's Art Exhibition

Vision: a cowboy's spur digs into a horse.
We witches are losing hair over this - fetch the wigs!
A rival spell must we prepare for those two:
gloom, tragedy, and melancholy -
these shall fall upon Grendel the foe!
Wildly the cauldron crackled and bumbled!
All who entered Grendel's art exhibition...
were left reduced and heartbroken to the core!
A man grabbed Gayowulf's shoulder:
look around you - look at all of this art!
Grendel's artwork alone is enough to destroy a man!

Book I: Section III: Canto VI: Grendel's Broken Arm

Vision: a wolf leering at a bathing swan.
Our divination confirms it: Grendel must die!
Let us scry: ah, Gayowulf approaches Grendel...
Come, Gayowulf, away to my secret room -
Grendel then led Gayowulf into his art studio.
A granite self - portrait was unveiled by Grendel!
Recall, witches, that if the two kiss, our magick prevails!
Gayowulf dropped to his knees: Grendel, marry me!
Grendel agreed, and leaned in for a kiss -
Gayowulf's strong lips threw Grendel backwards:
he fell into and broke off the arm from his self - portrait!

BOOK II: GRENDEL'S MOMMY

The Rainbow Cantos

Book II: Section I: Canto I: Bathroom Nervous Breakdown

Vision: a caught fish flopping on the deck of a boat.
Flailing, Grendel took the broken arm and ran:
he saw Gayowulf for the last time, in that state.
Grendel arrived at his mommy's abode;
once there, he darted to the bathroom:
chugging vodka, he locked himself in!
Because of Gayowulf, I broke my magnum opus...
He then took the arm and smashed the mirror!
In the cabinet he found what he sought:
a bottle full of Xanax: he took every last one...
His mommy burst in: Grendel died in her arms!

Book II: Section I: Canto II: Grendel's Open Casket Adieu

Grendel would always say: one must be apathetic!
Eyes closed and hands - folded Grendel lay there ~
it seems as if he ~ as if he ~...
as if he were only just resting, and still alive,
instead of sitting alongside flowers in a casket...
Gone fades Grendel into the night: away he goes!
Gayowulf flinched and fell back onto his knees:
farewell, great lover and love of mine! Adieu!
Next in the funeral service would come a song:
a requiem sung by Grendel's mommy.
Gayowulf had never met Grendel's mommy before.

Book II: Section I: Canto III: Requiem For Grendel

Vision: a hedgehog surrounded by wolves.
Witches! Grendel's mommy begins her song:
the crystal ball reveals a woman dressed all in black!
Old foe, we spy upon you now:
Grendel is gone, and you are next!
Spotlights centered on Mommy, and she began!
Oh, such a somber requiem she sings for her son!
Focus, witches, observe the prey of Gayowulf:
she was once an honored witch of Freyja:
now she performs the rites of Hecate!
Mommy's requiem evoked a standing ovation!

Book II: Section I: Canto IV: A Reception Most Inceptive

Grendel in his coffin: as beautiful as ever!
Even in death does Grendel mask his face:
forever dressed as if ready for a masquerade ball...
Gayowulf's tears rusted his iron heart for a change:
Grendel's demise deprived Gayowulf of a true love!
Mommy said: I believe you knew my son Grendel...
I hear you are a man with many talents, Gayowulf:
a bold fashion student eager to make his mark!
Tell you what ~ I may have a job for you:
come have tea at my Park Avenue apartment!
Then the famous soul singer withdrew into the crowd...

Book II: Section I: Canto V: Park Avenue Menagerie

Vision: the intricate den of a female black widow spider...
Witches! Gather round the crystal ball:
Gayowulf knocks at the door of Grendel's mommy!
Come in! Welcome to my little menagerie:
count if you can the four cats and three dogs!
Gayowulf sat and lounged in Mommy's loveseat...
Mommy stood up: Gayowulf I need you...
What is wealth or fame without a son!
You will report to my Park Avenue apartment weekly:
first, I shall try you as a personal seamstress...
Happy to gain an influential patron, Gayowulf accepted!

Book II: Section I: Canto VI: Call Me Mommy

Vision: a boa constrictor hugging a mouse to sleep...
Come near to me, Gayowulf! Listen closely to my words:
these past few months have been hard upon us both!
Grendel's absence has left a void in my life ~
but you fill that gap, Gayowulf, without a doubt!
I have lost a son, but how I have gained another one!
Come nearer to me, Gayowulf, feel no restraint:
share in this life that I have worked so hard to build!
My adopted son! My boyish muse! Oh, Gayowulf:
you must drop at once all formalities with me:
henceforward you shall call me Mommy!

Book II: Section II: Canto I: Birth Of Grendel's Mommy

Vision: a mother lamb nursing a stray lion cub...
Chant, Weird Sisters! Now we astro - project:
let us go back and view Mommy's fated birth!
Once our sister, she was excommunicated:
she ran off and joined a Hecate cult...
Blessed by Freyja at birth, now she is cursed!
Even as a child had she the strongest of voices:
in no time at all she rose to power and fame!
Marked at birth, we all should have known:
such an omen foretold her future, most dark!
Yet the prophecy holds: Mommy must die!

Book II: Section II: Canto II: Dance Of The Nude Occultists

Vision: a glass of milk fallen over...
Dear Gayowulf: you will report to Central Park
at midnight on the dot. From there, follow the path -
in more ways than one! Greet me tonight!
Prepare to see your Mommy in a fresh new light!
A roaring fire cast shadows on the nude occultists...
Come into the circle, Gayowulf! Join in our dance!
Gayowulf stripped and took Mommy by the hand:
our bond is stronger now than ever before!
Twirling around the fire the occultists began to chant:
hail Hecate, the true Goddess of all witches!

Book II: Section II: Canto III: Bath Of The High Priestess

It's been a while since I had my last bath:
how about you come over today after school lets out?
Sounds good, Mommy! Be there in a jiffy!
Now let's get down to business, Suzy Q!
Ready your arm: just like always, alright?
Mommy jabbed a syringe into Suzy Q's arm…
that should be enough: here's your money.
Mommy wasted no time in drawing up her bath:
better than botox, her ritual works wonders!
What was Mommy's secret? She'll never tell…
nothing fights wrinkles like soaking in virgin's blood!

Book II: Section II: Canto IV: Lactations Of Hecate

Garbed in the robes of a High Priestess, Mommy stood:
in the ritualistic chamber were two things:
an altar with an offering bowl, and a statue of Hecate…
What was the true cause of my son Grendel's death?
Hecate! Accept my offering! Give me a sign!
From Hecate's nips a creamy substance began to drip: milk!
So, I will have another son, after - all, then?
Answer me one more question, Queen of All Witches!
What of my adopted son and great love, Gayowulf:
shall he share the same fate as Grendel's father?
Explosively, Hecate's statue now flowed fresh blood…

Book II: Section II: Canto V: To The Fair Isle Of Mykonos

Near is the solstice! Duty calls!
Travel to the Temple of Hecate, I must:
there will I perform the ritual with Gayowulf!
How Gayowulf shall suspect nothing all the while:
I shall lull him into a false sense of security…
Journey with Mommy to the fair isle of Mykonos!
Be my personal fashion consultant for the trip:
dressing a star like me could really boost your career!
Gayowulf agreed: Mommy I am coming with you!
Stellar! We must pack our belongings immediately:
thus begins our pilgrimage to the Temple of Hecate!

The Rainbow Cantos
Book II: Section II: Canto VI: All Aboard The S. S. Oscar Wilde

Vision: a matron undertakes one final voyage...
Up the steps ascended Gayowulf and Mommy:
they boarded the S. S. Oscar Wilde cruise!
Opulent was everything on that boat:
Mommy could only ever travel in style, after - all!
Full speed ahead to the Grecian isles!
Mommy ~ what business do you have in Greece?
I know you journey to the Temple of Hecate...
Mommy answered: because the solstice nears!
Shh, Gayowulf ~ trouble me no more with your inquiries:
not every question of yours needs an answer!

Book II: Section III: Canto I: Gayowulf Has A Night Tremor

Vision: the mommy of the Colossus of Rhodes...
Witches! We are in the endgame, now...
Gayowulf functions as the bait for our trap!
We Weird Sisters strike with impunity -
Mommy shall never step foot in Greece!
Live or die, Gayowulf will have fulfilled his purpose...
with his life will we take a chance and roll the dice!
We Weird Sisters must now go to ready our spell:
off to the garden, to gather magickal herbs...
Gayowulf woke - up sweating in his cabin:
his night tremor filled him with a sense of dread...

Book II: Section III: Canto II: Mommy's Secret Whispers

Vision: a succulent roast ham on Christmas day...
Almost time for dinner: Gayowulf would fetch Mommy.
Down the cruise hall Gayowulf ambled along:
moments before he knocked at Mommy's door -
Gayowulf heard whispers coming from inside!
I am en route with the flesh sacrifice!
Your High Priestess arrives in a week;
no, no, he suspects nothing: a perfect lamb!
First Gayowulf must give me a son...
and then will I perform the Ritual of the Mantis...
Baa! Baa! How Gayowulf is a perfect lamb!

Book II: Section III: Canto III: Gayowulf Has A Panic Attack

Vision: an oyster farmed for its pearl...
Gayowulf's sanity came crashing down:
to his room he retreated: what comes next?
He took a medallion out of his suitcase -
a mysterious token found in his cradle:
Gayowulf rubbed the coin in a frenzy!
Just then the Weird Sisters were jolted:
Gayowulf is in trouble: he needs our help!
How Mommy wishes to carve me up!
Panic overcame Gayowulf: truly am I lost!
A knock came at his door: it was Mommy...

The Rainbow Cantos

Book II: Section III: Canto IV: Coitus A La Praying Mantis

Vision: a squirrel sleeping amidst a forest fire...
Gayowulf awoke in a pitch - black room:
Mommy walked in and turned on the lights.
Awake now, Gayowulf? Have a nice sleep?
Gayowulf discovered himself naked and tied - up!
Now you shall suffer the fate of Grendel's father!
First comes copulation, then comes prayer:
then comes your own decapitation, Gayowulf!
Are you satisfied with that? All hail Hecate!
Mommy prepared herself for the ritual:
Gayowulf would yield her a son most fine!

Book II: Section III: Canto V: Bibbity Bobbity Boom

Vision: Pompei before the volcanic eruption...
Bibbity bobbity boo! Bibbity bobbity boom!
Be alert, witches: now comes the end for Mommy!
Into the cauldron went many toxic chemicals:
flames and sparks rustled inside, gaining momentum!
Let the S. S. Oscar Wilde meet a fiery doom!
With each chant more damage was done to the ship:
Gayowulf freed himself and ran up to the main deck!
Mommy chased after him yelling and screaming:
we must finish the ritual, Gayowulf, come back!
One final time the witches sang: bibbity bobbity boom!

Book II: Section III: Canto VI: Into The Depths Fades Mommy

Boom! Boom! Crash! Boom! Boom!
Fire! Fire! Water! Fire! Fire!
There sank that ship into the ocean blue:
hundreds of miles away from the shore!
Suddenly the engine of the boat exploded:
night closed in on the S. S. Oscar Wilde...
Some dived off the ship as it sank:
but Gayowulf commandeered a lifeboat!
In the distance the Oscar Wilde submerged...
Out of the water shot Mommy's arm:
Gayowulf dodged it and Mommy went down under...

BOOK III: THE KIMONO DRAGON

The Rainbow Cantos

Book III: Section I: Canto I: Fall Of The House Of Gayowulf

Vision: a losing lottery ticket...
Our company is down on the stock market:
people are not buying Gayowulf like they used to!
As a fashion brand it got too big too fast:
after Gayowulf inherited Mommy's money -
he started his own fashion design firm!
Gayowulf stood up at the meeting:
I vow to never allow House Gayowulf to fail!
We are in debt: how will you fix that?
I will have to take on new elite clients!
Gayowulf sat down gazing out the window...

Book III: Section I: Canto II: Triple Shot Macchiato

To whom must Gayowulf turn in his desperation?
Wiglaf wondered that as he got Gayowulf's drink:
one triple shot venti iced macchiato and make it snappy!
He then hustled back to that regular Milan warehouse,
where Gayowulf spent his laboring hours of the day...
How would Gayowulf avoid declaring bankruptcy?
Wiglaf worried about his own livelihood and future, too...
He served after - all as Gayowulf's personal assistant:
he knew all of Gayowulf's virtues and all of his vices...
Wiglaf entered the office: here is your macchiato!
Then Wiglaf prepared to give Gayowulf a foot massage...

Book III: Section I: Canto III: Mopey Dopey Milan Overdose

Vision: a cat crossing a major highway...
Gayowulf felt the blues: he had a hunger:
it was time to cook: Gayowulf's body agreed:
a powder most fine was placed atop the spoon:
his torch - lighter warmed the spoon's underside:
fluid entered the syringe then Gayowulf's arm:
blood and heroin mixed together pleasurably:
Gayowulf slumped forward in his chair:
he had injected a lethal dose this time:
now he foamed bubbles at the mouth:
it had been six months since his last overdose...

Book III: Section I: Canto IV: Aim For The Heart, Wiglaf

Vision: a waterless goldfish outside of its tank...
Wiglaf opened the door and found Gayowulf:
Jesus fucking Christ! Just look at him!
He's got no fucking self - control, as ever!
What did Gayowulf say in case of emergencies?
Aim for the heart, Wiglaf! Keep a level head!
Gayowulf was a man of many talents:
but assuredly moderation wasn't one of them...
Okey dokey, sighed Wiglaf, as he opened the kit:
he hovered the adrenaline shot above Gayowulf:
stab! Gayowulf woke up: did you get my macchiato?

Book III: Section I: Canto V: Seal Of The Kimono Dragon

Vision: a jackpot is won on a slot machine...
After his overdose, Gayowulf's mood worsened:
the bankruptcy of his fashion house loomed...
Wiglaf, give me some good news for a change!
Well, a gilded parchment scroll arrived by courier:
it bears a glittering seal: of a robed dragon, sir!
Gayowulf broke the seal and began reading:
Dear Gayowulf: I am a retired businessman:
I hail from a nation most honorable: Japan;
restyle my palace, and I'll pay $ 25, 000, 000:
I'll expect your arrival... Signed, Kimono

Book III: Section I: Canto VI: One Last Dragon To Chase

Dream: a tornado full of poppy flowers...
Wiglaf! Make the arrangements for our voyage:
an odyssey across the ocean to the realm of Japan!
Before you do any of that: fetch me another macchiato!
Gayowulf opened his desk after Wiglaf left the office:
from within it he grabbed that which he craved...
So, who the fuck is this Kimono Dragon character?
He lit the spoon as usual: the syringe was readied...
What kind of sucker is willing to pay $ 25, 000, 000?
Heroin entered his system: he wondered one last thing...
What am I gonna buy myself with all of Kimono's cash?

The Rainbow Cantos

Book III: Section II: Canto I: Gayowulf And Wiglaf Arrive In Japan

Saying: even a crane can fly out of a dumpster...
Waves beat against the ship as it harbored:
Tokyo Bay lay straight ahead: Wiglaf smiled...
Gayowulf grabbed Wiglaf by the shoulder:
we are here for one reason alone, do not forget:
to earn the $ 25, 000, 000 and get the fuck out!
Wipe that smile off your face: wake the hell up!
Demonstrate your loyalty to me by doing your job:
you know that my addiction eats away at my soul:
keep me intact throughout this endeavor -
if I make it out of Japan alive, you'll be rewarded!

Book III: Section II: Canto II: Ready, Set, Go - Go

Vision: butterflies entering into a web of sin...
Tokyo faded from view as they rounded Mount Fuji:
a driver had picked them up adjacent the docks...
For a while they drove into the countryside;
suddenly the chauffeur turned into a large wood:
Wiglaf eyed a sign and read it: Aokigahara Forest...
Next, they reached a fenced gate: hold the phone!
Gayowulf was astonished by the guardswoman:
she was a beauty to behold, in full uniform:
her kimono aptly clashed with her go - go boots;
slung over her shoulder was a pink machine gun!

Book III: Section II: Canto III: Palace Of The Kimono Dragon

Gayowulf and Wiglaf arrived at the palace:
in the foyer a Kimono Guard greeted them:
remove your clothes: proper attire is required:
the two men slipped into exquisite kimonos...
Come this way: the Dragon himself nears!
A gong was rung, and a sliding door opened:
his kimono was most glorious to behold!
Greetings Gayowulf: I am the Kimono Dragon!
As you can see, privacy matters a lot to me;
supper is in an hour: go now to your rooms...
Kimono left them and returned to his chambers.

Book III: Section II: Canto IV: If His Kimono Could Talk

Vision: a hammer smashes a marble statue...
Playing in the background was a string quartet:
Kimono rang a bell and addressed the dinner table:
his kimono bore tigers and florals all across it:
we welcome today Mister Gayowulf to my palace:
here he will redecorate my splendorous estate!
Wiglaf nudged Gayowulf and he became alert:
thank you, most dazzling Kimono Dragon!
He then received a flirty glance from Kimono!
What is this man's story? Who is he?
Who is the Kimono Dragon? Gayowulf sighed...

Book III: Section II: Canto V: Off Comes The Kimono For Gayowulf

Vision: the mating of two rabid hyenas...
A thousand candles lit up Kimono's bedroom:
Gayowulf and Kimono lounged sipping cognac...
Your palace is so ornate, mused Gayowulf:
how could you want me to remodel it all?
Kimono turned serious: I have watched from afar:
my eye is keen to spot the next big designer...
and I think your fashion style is superlative!
Your words land close to my heart, Kimono:
however, I cannot help but wonder this:
did you summon me to Japan just to seduce me?
Kimono loosened his kimono: it gently slid off.

Book III: Section II: Canto VI: Flames Of The Kimono Dragon

Vision: the sharp pincers of a scorpion...
Months flew by while Gayowulf worked:
most of the palace was redecorated, now!
Passion and need drove Gayowulf's days:
exhaustion and haze colored Gayowulf's nights,
for: Kimono was a dragon most insatiable!
Nevertheless, Gayowulf yearned to leave:
his Italian Greyhounds remained in Milan!
Yet something did not bode well in Japan:
it seemed as if Kimono were a manic volcano...
who knew what may trigger his eruption?

The Rainbow Cantos

Book III: Section III: Canto I: The Kimono Dragon Serves Hibachi

Vision: a gourmet chef poisons his tasty creation...
Tonight, I will be cooking dinner, said Kimono:
it shall be Hibachi: I figure we might as well...
try things the American way, for a change!
This evening my chief Kimono Guard joins us;
Kimono began to chop, to twirl, and to fry:
suddenly he raised his spatula up in the air:
he slammed it down on his chief guard's wrist,
slicing the guard's hand off instantaneously!
This man betrayed me! Take him away, guards!
And take Gayowulf and Wiglaf back to their rooms!

Book III: Section III: Canto II: Intentions Of The Dragon Revealed

Kimono spoke: let me tell you why you are here...
Every few years I begin to miss my former life:
as a retired Prince of the International Black Market,
I made my fame and fortune as a brutal gangster -
I miss the intrigue but most of all: the danger!
True, I did want my palace renovated by you, but:
ulterior motives lured you to Japan and into my trap...
Let me ask: do you like to gamble, Gayowulf and Wiglaf?
Complete three challenges and earn your freedom!
First: sew for me a kimono worthy of the Dragon...
Second: groove on my Disco Dance Floor of Death...
Third: out - snort me while playing Cocaine Roulette...

Book III: Section III: Canto III: A Kimono Worthy Of The Dragon

Vision: a work of art awaiting critical claws...
Bolted was the door: a Kimono Guard paced outside;
Wiglaf began to lose sight of any chance of hope:
he broke down: will I make it out of here alive?
Shut the fuck up, Wiglaf! Gayowulf was busy:
he cradled in his hands his most fabulous work yet!
Demand another macchiato from the guard!
How Gayowulf sewed a miracle to save them both:
a turquoise kimono littered with gilded cranes!
Kimono was brought to tears by its embroidery:
Gayowulf and Wiglaf would live to see another day!

Book III: Section III: Canto IV: Disco Dance Floor of Death

Vision: Sisyphus rolling his rock uphill...
Next Kimono took them to a special room:
mirrored panels were fixed to the walls:
in the middle of the room hung a disco ball...
Here, you must dance to save your lives!
Kimono withdrew into a control room:
welcome to my Disco Dance Floor of Death!
Laser beams shot out of the disco ball:
Gayowulf and Wiglaf danced to avoid them!
Then the floor opened: an electric eel tank!
Both men boogied away from the opening:
Kimono was satisfied and let them live...

Book III: Section III: Canto V: Gayowulf Attempts Cocaine Roulette

Vision: two people playing Russian Roulette...
Kimono led Gayowulf and Wiglaf into a room:
sit down, my captives: listen here, now!
Play and win Cocaine Roulette against me:
if you beat me, you leave with the $ 25, 000, 000!
The rules are simple: we shall snort in turns...
whoever is first to overdose, loses everything!
Gayowulf and Kimono snorted one after the other:
eventually Gayowulf lost his will to carry on:
he overdosed, fell over, and then died...
Wiglaf shouted: I will avenge Gayowulf!

Book III: Section III: Canto VI: Wiglaf Out-Snorts The Kimono Dragon

Vision: the light at the end of the tunnel...
Kimono took a powder room break to collect himself:
Wiglaf, too, would face off against the Dragon...
Kimono jingled a dainty bell: bring out the cocaine!
Wiglaf's reason to out - snort the Kimono Dragon was:
back at his place he had a gimp to take care of!
Now Wiglaf really readied himself for battle:
I shall go first! Wiglaf then snortéd a hefty line...
But Kimono did not go down without a fight:
he kept Wiglaf on his toes to the bitter end:
when Wiglaf triumphed, he yelled: for Gayowulf!

G. R. Tomaini is an LGBTQ Federal McNair Scholar. His academic monograph on Philosophy, Beyond Analytic Philosophy: Introducing a System of American Idealism is forthcoming from Manticore Press; one of his four full-length poetry manuscripts was recently accepted for publication by A Thin Slice of Anxiety Press ~ Ballad of An American Ganymede; the work consists of 57 poems in the manner of Queer Existentialist Poetry inspired by Heidegger and Sartre. Two of his other books of poetry recently have been accepted for publication by Pumpernickel Press, to be published jointly under the title: The Rainbow Cantos: Two Attempts At Queering The Canon; the two books of poetry that have been accepted are Kiss Me, Ahab! and Gayowulf. Tomaini's poems are featured in Outcast Press's magazine, Selcouth Station Press's journal, and in a mini-volume by The Incognito Press. For more information visit: www.grtomaini.com of follow him on twitter at GTomaini.

The Rainbow Cantos

 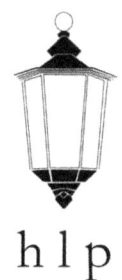 

p h   h l p   B A B

Pumpernickel House Publishing is a family of independent journals and presses based out of New Orleans, LA. Pumpernickel House, the parent-press, publishes fairy tales, magical realism, and fabulism. Black Annis Books is an imprint focused on socially-concious and feminist horror. Half-Light Press is an imprint focused on hybrid works, speculative fiction, and works that explore the margins between genres. We strive to promote not just our own work, but the work of all within the indie author community. We want to make art, writing, and lit accessible to all, and give all authors and publishers a space for their voices, and a hand up. We want to take academia out of the academy and make it, literary conversation, and creative writing education accessible to all. To do so, we hold indie-author promotional events, teach affordable, virtual creative writing classes, and plan and host the annual Half-Light Lit Fest and Conference every January in New Orleans.

For more information, visit www.pumpernickelhouse.com

www.ingramcontent.com/pod-product-compliance
Lightning Source LLC
LaVergne TN
LVHW012024060526
838201LV00061B/4449